JEAN COCTEAU

Vive la jeune
Muse
Cinéma
Car elle
possède
le mystère
du rêve
et permet de
rendre l'irréalité
réaliste
Jean Cocteau ~ 1959

JEAN COCTEAU

by René Gilson

TRANSLATED BY CIBA VAUGHAN

Editions Seghers' Cinéma d'Aujourd'hui in English

Crown Publishers, Inc., New York

General editor of the Collection Cinéma d'Aujourd'hui: Pierre Lherminier
Cover designed by Leonard Cascioli
Cover photo of Jean Cocteau: From *Testament of Orpheus,* released by Brandon
Films, Inc.

Acknowledgments

Our thanks for their assistance in the preparation of this volume to Mme. Janine André-Bazin, Mme. Fernande Lillette, Henri Agel, Jean-Pierre Bastide, Jean-Louis Bory, A.-J. Cauliez, Jean Marais, Chris Marker, Sacha Mansour, André Maurois, André Paulvé, Jacques Rivette, the Fédération Française des Ciné-Clubs, the Library of the I.D.H.E.C., and the journals *Cinéma 64* and *Cahiers du Cinéma*.

Our thanks also to the publishing houses Editions André Bonne, Editions du Cerf, Editions Clairefontaine, Editions Gallimard, Editions du Rocher, Editions du Seuil, and Editions de la Table Ronde, who have given us authorization to use various texts to which they hold the copyright.

CONTENTS

JEAN COCTEAU:

An Essay by René Gilson

TEXTS

Chosen by René Gilson

THE CINEMA ACCORDING TO JEAN COCTEAU

ILLUSTRATIONS

JEAN COCTEAU
An Essay by René Gilson

"The common herd will call you mad."
—RONSARD

"Then he felt a dreadful blow on the chest. He fell. He became deaf and blind. —'A bullet,' he said to himself. 'I am lost unless I pretend to be dead.' But in him, fiction and reality were one and the same. William Thomas was dead."
—COCTEAU, *Thomas l'Imposteur*

Death and the Young Man

"For a long time I have been preparing myself for the exercise which consists, for the poet, in simulating death." In the fourth episode of *The Blood of a Poet*, Cocteau's first film, the poet dies, the statue becomes a statue once again, and the poet's own creation is, in the end, going to replace him. The audience applauds. It is the same with poets as it once was with Indians in the Old West: The only good poet is a dead poet. Successively wounded seven times, Jean Cocteau lost his seven best friends. Above all, the four dyings of Roland Garros, Jean Le

11

Roy, Raymond Radiguet, and Jean Desbordes—chosen beings, his other selves—killed Cocteau four times over.

> "Make me accept a little the fact
> that my poor friend Jean has been killed."

From a 1920 poem, a hymn to the sun.

On his return to the cinema in 1942 [1] to write the script for *The Phantom Baron,* he insisted—to the great dismay of Paul Eluard—on playing the role of the baron during the latter's brief appearance in the Prologue; the baron, through whom Cocteau braves death and crumbles into dust. In *Testament of Orpheus,* [2] Cocteau plays himself; he is pierced by the lance of Minerva, and falls. But this is only one among the poet's many deaths, for he still has time to sound the call to battle, to rework the good and bad turns of fate, to compose his great *Testament,* and to answer his judges before his actual death. The 11th of October, 1963, this heart, which is recorded on the soundtrack of *The Blood of a Poet*—"this inimitable clamor, ferocious, nocturnal, impossibly complex"—stopped beating.

An Approach to a Portrait

Although Cocteau's last film, *Testament of Orpheus,* preserves for us his last face, and even though the extraordinary television production "Portrait-Souvenir" is still fresh in recollection, the portraits of Cocteau by Marie Laurencin and Modigliani, the photographs of him by Man Ray, and a 1933 self-portrait will, in mutual

---

[1] Cocteau's first film was *The Blood of a Poet,* in 1930, and he had no further contact with the cinema for twelve years.—ED.

[2] Cocteau's last film, 1960.

relationship, limn our particular portrait of the artist. The portrait by Marie Laurencin and the photographs by Man Ray reveal the sort of beauty that Cocteau believed he did not possess: a delicate subtlety and certain firmness in his features, a black vivacity of an unexpected Spanishness in the hair, the eyes, and the eyebrows. Modigliani, on the other hand, caught a certain physical malaise; he paints Cocteau as the peasant of Paris, dressed up in Sunday clothes like Margaritis in *Atalante* . . . flowing bowtie, a certain stiffness and strain in the body and its pose, the neck stretched a bit awkwardly . . . the asymmetric features (a quality Cocteau loved in architecture), an extraordinary foreshadowing of the future deformation of the nose, lines that are long and extended but neither weak nor dissolute, audaciously lively angles that do not cut. As Colette said in *The Blue Lantern,* speaking of Cocteau, her neighbor in the Palais-Royal, "His angular grace bruises nothing." And through all these details one perceives the profound essence of the man, perfectly grasped and articulated by a painter of genius: all the gravity, the seriousness, the anxiety, the professional conscientiousness of the craftsman, the laborer. But above all the malaise. "We live in a dangerous visibility," Cocteau would say. He openly acknowledged this malaise—which existed in back of his elegance that was so visible, yet which he could not feel—in the self-portrait of *The Difficulty of Being.*

Certainly no one could have felt more than Cocteau the need to have several bodies and to change among them at will. He must have felt the desire, too, like his character Jacques Forestier in *Grand Ecart,* "to be those whom he found beautiful. . . . His own beauty displeased him. He found it ugly." Hence the self-portrait, sketched in 1933, which is diametrically opposed to the portrait by Modigliani, and which, in its beauty, goes even beyond the beauty that he refused to recognize in the Man Ray photographs and in the portrait by Marie Laurencin. In his own drawing, the expression, the nose, and the chin affirm the confidence and strength of a virile beauty reminiscent of the heroes in Murnau's American films. Idealizing himself—unconsciously, surely—in this sketch that is intended to be his own face. Jean Cocteau seems to incorporate therein all that he admired and would have liked to appropriate in the faces of Dargelos, Roland Garros, and Radiguet, and, later, in the faces of Jean Marais and Edouard Dermit. Here we find the same features that later, in lines more supple, troubling, Greek, Cocteau would fix definitively in the face of a young man, a face he was to sketch with obsession and profusion to the end of his life; a face that incarnated for him the lyre and the muse, Eros and Agape, the platonic Ideal of Beauty, "the supernatural sex of beauty." [1]

It seems appropriate at this point, then—and especially if we are to understand the cinematic work of Jean Cocteau, which is the least flippant or fantastical creation imaginable—to assemble another, more truthful, picture of the artist. We must do away with the intellectual catchwords that are too often used to describe him: Cocteau the bold and brilliant, the prestidigitator, the spellbinder, the sorcerer. Cocteau never indulged in sleight of hand. Whether on film, in the theatre, faced with the pages or the white walls of his poems written or sketched, he never had tricks up his sleeve. In the cinema, particularly, he is not Merlin the magician, but one of those who claims affinity with Méliès rather than with Lumière, who prefers the realities of theatre to the lifeless recording of reality. The pain in the life of this least frivolous of men, who was to live with heart held open and pierced by the lance of a goddess of false reason, effectively gives the lie to the lies that infest the Cocteau legend. Above all, it is the gravity, the naked sincerity, the kindness of heart, the predilection for, and the love of, friendship and work—and the vital need he had of these—that define him most clearly. To write, sketch, or film—in short, to create—was an act of love for him, a way of life, the gift of self and the search for self, an offertory to the public, but never alms: Cocteau never played to the gallery.

Finally, before abandoning this outline of a portrait (the study of Cocteau's work will fill it in much more satisfactorily), one must protest, with only the necessary minimum of ill will, Jean-Paul Sartre's calling Cocteau a "prince of counterfeit"—"counterfeiter whom I love," Sartre hastened to add. One might be tempted to return the same phrase to

[1] All citations without footnotes are from Jean Cocteau.

Sartre, whose counterfeit theatre, counterfeit novels, and cantilevered politics have so seduced us. Today, against that *encyclopédiste* and the uncertain future of his paper money, I choose the fine gold of the honest sovereigns of the poet.

Approaches to a Mystery

Or the evident realities of a mystery.

Jean Cocteau and cinematography.

A number of years ago, when those young filmmakers to whom we owe the recent revolution in the French film were still preparing themselves for their craft by critical examination of the cinema, several of them selected as mentors, or at least as admired examples (in addition to the American masters), five living French filmmakers. This group of five (or of six, for René Clément should be—or might have been—among them, but I like the number five, and Jean-Paul Melville belongs more to the new school of cinematographers) consisted of Jean Renoir, Max Ophüls, Jacques Becker, Jean Cocteau, and Robert Bresson. Neither Max Ophüls nor Jacques Becker finished his love affair with the cinema; they died in anguish. But God saved the rest. Jean Cocteau, man of the poetic order, was able to make his final testament, and for this testament he chose—as he said, and as Jean Renoir still says— cinematography.

Jean Cocteau lived poetic experience through the words of his poems, novels, and plays, through dance and through mime drama, through the lines and forms of his drawings and frescoes, and through the cinema. Although he first entered into the creation of films with ease, with a freshness of spirit and invention, and without presumption (with *The Blood of a Poet* in 1930), Jean Cocteau afterward waited through a long period of maturation, if you will, rather than of apprenticeship (though he did not disdain the latter), before finally adopting the cinema as a new vehicle for his poetry. After a hiatus of fifteen years, Cocteau made his commitment to the cinema in 1945, with the production of *Beauty and the Beast.* From that moment, the cinema became the means through which he could capture his world and its myths most concretely, most fully; catching everything up in his arms, he was able to embrace the most riches in a single sweep, and at the same time give the most of himself. Throughout the one hundred and fifty pages of *The Difficulty of Being,* he continually and with obvious preference refers to his films: eight times to *The Blood of a Poet,* twelve times to *Beauty and the Beast.* One senses in this book, written in 1947, that Cocteau is living a great new beginning, that of the "poetry of cinema"—as he used to speak of the "poetry of theatre" and the "poetry of the novel"—the beginning of his cinematic creativity, magnificently controlled and carried to heights of splendor in *Beauty and the Beast.*

It is through the marvelous (we shall hear more of the marvelous later, and of Cocteau's contention that films like *The Blood of a Poet, Beauty and the Beast,* and *Orpheus* are as realistic as *Les Parents terribles*[1]) that Jean Cocteau, after the cautious first steps of *The Phantom Baron* (1943) and *The Eternal Return* (1943),[2] entered triumphantly and definitively into the cinema. But this "marvelous" is not the easy, childish "fantastic"; it is, rather, an affirmation of rigor and of order. Cocteau did not deliberately invoke the marvelous in his films; for one thing, he did not know exactly where to find it, nor where it awaited him; most of the time he simply bumped into it, and stopped short. By the same token, the spectator is not obliged to track down either the marvelous or the poetic in Cocteau's films; one does not have to try to ferret them out. One descends straight, down the length of the "mystery perpendicular to the discourse" in a Cocteau film. He loved right angles, and "the plumb line became [his]

---

[1] Which did not prevent Cocteau from saying elsewhere *"Les Parents terribles* is not a realistic film, since I've never known a family to live like that."

[2] Cocteau was responsible for the dialogues in these two films, but he had no significant role in their direction.—ED.

favorite means of locomotion." One descends straight and fast, gripped by a kind of vertigo, captive, toward the spell; the film works on us, draws us into its zone, where we find the conviction, affirmation, certainty, and plenitude of poetry. Certainty, for never once are we solicited by the use of sentimental, poetical, or esthetic drivel to move toward emotion, poetry, beauty. False poetry fraught with symbols, vague, ornamental, or irreal for its own sake does not exist in Cocteau's work; when the irreal is taken up, it becomes realistic. This is poetry of precision. In the final analysis, one recognizes Cocteau as a poet of the cinema, not by his "style," but by the purity and naïveté of his gaze. The word "naïveté," in this regard, is invested with the freshness and force of its best sense, a sense that has been disfigured by certain confusions stemming from painting. Here is the naïveté of the quick and audacious, unfettered intelligence of childhood, but at the service of a man. No one enters into Cocteau's universe if he be not possessed of this naïveté, this freshness of soul and of childhood retained. It is this quality the poet demands of us in the prologue of *Beauty and the Beast;* a quality that is not unknowingness, but is that by which Cocteau recognized, "by an assortment of singular naïvetés which the plural disproves," that Rousseau was almost a poet. It is also the naïveté of the crew on his films, always delighted to see him again. "Ah! Monsieur Cocteau, it's just not *Beauty and the Beast,* you know, so we're bored—all these other films are just like the stories we hear from our wives." Cocteau never failed to bring them to the rushes, and always marveled at their delighted surprise to see coherent images take form from the apparently unorganized elements they had helped to film.

The above also illustrates the warmth-in-work climate in which Cocteau's films were made, an atmosphere from which he took pleasure. Cocteau loved to work; he dug his hands into the dough, coming and going, thinking, animating, discussing, grappling with practical problems, improvising solutions with the help of an inventive crew. His crew cared for Cocteau, and he cared for and respected them.

In the "journal" of *Beauty and the Beast* [1] he continually celebrates the

1 *La Belle et la Bête, Journal d'un film,* Editions du Rocher, Paris.

merit of his crew and the comfort he drew from their moral and professional worth, from their attentions and kindnesses during the production
of a film that was, for its creator, a passion in both senses of the term: a
terrible battle against incessant material difficulties, and an all-consuming
mania. He was aware of, and admired, the fact that at any moment he
could ask the impossible of his crew and they would answer, "It can be
done." One hour afterward, planks, saws, hammers, nails, and ingenuity—
that is to say, the special genius of their trade—would yield up to the master
of the enterprise the material possibilities with which to put his idea into
practice. He admired this band of artisans knowledgeably at the service of
artistic creation, and considered that his own work as author of the film was
that of a skilled manual laborer through whom the spirit took shape. "A
trade well done fascinates me," he used to say, watching a sound-effects
man at work, enchanted with the latter's gadgets and the pleasure he takes
in doing this bizarre job well. But with what profound joy did he himself
perform his task of cinematic creation, even when forced, as during the
filming of *Beauty and the Beast,* to overcome dreadful pain and to push
his physical and emotional endurance to impossible limits. During the filming of his last movie, *Testament of Orpheus,* François-Régis Bastide (a
friend of both Louis Aragon and Jean Cocteau, and sent by the former as
a reporter, or rather as a visitor, on behalf of *Les Lettres françaises*) was
horrified to see Cocteau burn up the hours when he should have been
asleep, and he cried, "Such mad imprudence; he's endangering himself."

Jean Cocteau, then, was not a passive admirer of the ingenious work
from which he profited. He, from personal necessity, continually paid with
his person. It was not a dabbler who clambered over all the ladders, cat-
walks, and props, searing his eyes beneath the spotlights. He had to live
in the set, to sense himself how one might live it, in order to bring his
characters to life in it afterward. He often felt the need to set the scene
himself. During *Beauty and the Beast,* for example, he needed to spread
out and arrange the sheets in the orchard of Beauty's father himself, to
construct in his own design the perspective of winding white lanes. His
friends—and, one must believe, many directors as well—didn't understand
how Jean Cocteau could give so much of himself, indeed, give all of him-

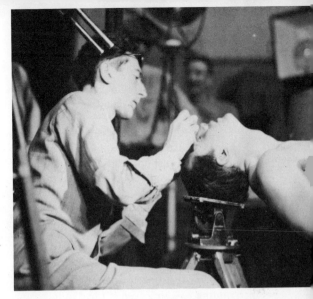

Jean Cocteau and Enrique Rivero during production of *The Blood of a Poet*.
Sacha Mansour

self, for a film. Jean Cocteau, for his part, could not understand how one could not give in this way to the work that one carries in oneself.

Between Jean Cocteau and his crew existed not only the intensity of friendship by which he was possessed and which he communicated to others; there was also a communion: "To live together, to work and discuss work, represented for me the height of luxury." This communion attained to even deeper definition during the period of intensive collaboration. From the first great film that Cocteau managed entirely by himself, *Beauty*, he knew how to impose the demands of his style, his boldness, and that sense of surety that cloaked his fears and secret anxieties. He knew—and his foreknowledge was the only precaution he would accept—the risks he was taking, even as he turned what he called the dead rules of cinematography upside down. And with every stroke he prevailed against the reticence, the habits, and the training of the professional filmmakers—of Alekan, Clément, Tiquet [1]—and against their own fears and anxieties, secret or not. He transmitted his spirit of admirable excess so feared by his

[1] Respectively: director of photography, technical adviser, and cameraman for *Beauty and the Beast*.

director of photography. But at night he would wake with a start, a forgotten continuity shot tormenting him; he would work out a correction, then say to himself: "I am not, perhaps I never will be, a real director. I am too caught up in what's happening; I watch, I attend the production, become the audience, and I forget the continuity shots." Which proves that he was indeed a real director, one of the finest. He knew how to quicken a scene, to give it a soul, because he lost his own soul in it; and the first part of his soul to go was the technician, just like Jean Renoir who was always the first to view his films and who also sometimes forgot continuity shots. He quickened his collaborators, communicating to them his enthusiasm and, in the long run, even his style. At one point during the filming of *Beauty and the Beast,* believing that illness and the violence of his pain were going to force him to leave the set for the second time, he wrote in his journal of the film: "It is true that, thanks to my crew, I would not be interrupting anything even if I had to interrupt my presence. Marais would survey the acting. Clément the direction, Ibéria the continuity.[1] Bédard would add the miracle. My machinery is solid enough to run for a week without me, on its own steam." He had succeeded in giving sufficient impulse and momentum to this machine.

"To move this great engine of dreams, to do battle with the angel of light . . . the angels of space and time, this is work to my measure. . . . I've done my best."

At the end of each film, Jean Cocteau was physically and emotionally exhausted from having given himself totally, with all his fidelity, all his honesty, all his strength. Genius was a part of that strength.

The singular cinematographic career of Jean Cocteau was constructed in three stages. In 1930 his friend the Vicomte Charles de Noailles gave him a million francs with which to make a film in complete freedom. (De Noailles gave the same gift to Luis Buñuel, who used the money to make *L'Age d'or*.) It is a curious irony, worth noting here, that when Cocteau tried to raise an equivalent sum in 1959 to produce his last film, *Testament of Orpheus,* the money was forthcoming with only the greatest

---

[1] Claude Ibéria, editor of the film.

difficulty, even though Cocteau was, at that time, at the height of his reputation as a filmmaker. Raoul Lévy declined; only the valiant efforts of some of the young film directors of the new French cinema—particularly François Truffaut and the producer Jean Thuillier—permitted *Testament* to be made.

The Blood of a Poet, filmed from April to September, 1930, in complete freedom and in complete innocence of the craft, was shown for the first time to the general public, introduced by Cocteau, at the Théâtre du Vieux-Colombier, on January 20, 1932. The film critics, as yet a rare breed, had already taken up their positions, following the private showings in 1931. Against: Louis Chavance. In *La Revue du Cinéma,* he spoke of "exasperated invention." For: Paul Gilson, who had seen the film from a poet's point of view, and was content merely to describe it in *Pour Vous.* Also against, and naturally with unbridled passion, were the surrealists, who in the confusion did succeed in passing the film off as surrealist, which it most assuredly was not. There was a lovely quarrel over *The Blood of a Poet.* But, afterward, there were, for a while, no more Cocteau films. Not because of the quarrel; on the contrary, it is likely that the uproar would rather have helped Cocteau to make another film, this time for commercial exploitation, had he wanted to. But filmmaking was not, at that time, his *métier.* The film was an experimental poem, a creation that had deeply excited the author: "Nothing is more beautiful than to write a poem with live beings, faces, hands, lights, and objects that one arranges as one likes." This poetry of the cinema couldn't be followed up—at least not immediately. *The Blood of a Poet* was the beginning and end of Stage I of Cocteau's film career.

During the thirties, Jean Cocteau was to write perhaps the very best of all that he was to give to theatre: *The Infernal Machine,* written in 1932 and produced in 1934; *King Oedipus* and *The Knights of the Round Table* in 1937, and *Les Parents terribles* in 1938. The second stage in this cinematographic development of Jean Cocteau was during the war years, a period of progressive ripening. During this time, he wrote for other directors, and followed their work. Then, in 1945, he decided to take upon himself alone the creation of *Beauty and the Beast,* and on the basis of this single great film he earned a place for himself among the foremost ranks of French filmmakers. *Beauty and the Beast* opens, then, the third stage. Works written or adapted by Jean Cocteau were still to be filmed by other directors: *Ruy Blas* with Pierre Billon, *The Human Voice* by Roberto Rossellini; and, later, after *Orpheus, Les Enfants terribles* by Jean-Pierre Melville. But Cocteau's situation was now different: He was no longer a dabbler in cinema; he had become a filmmaker. The major body of his work went forward from *Beauty and the Beast* (1945) to *L'Aigle à deux têtes* (1947), *Les Parents terribles* (1948), *Orpheus* (1950), and *Testament of Orpheus* (1960).

For our analysis of Cocteau's work, we shall consider his films, not in strict chronological order, but rather in terms of a different, and perhaps more organic, space-time sequence. The first natural grouping takes place during Cocteau's years as an "apprentice," when he learned the trade while writing screenplays and dialogues for the films of professional film-makers. *L'Aigle à deux têtes* is included here, even though Cocteau directed the film himself, because it has a certain rapport with *Ruy Blas*. Next come two extraordinary films, *Beauty and the Beast* and *Les Parents terribles*. The final grouping is three films widely separated in time—*The Blood of a Poet* (1930), *Orpheus* (1950), and *Testament of Orpheus* (1960)—which are linked in a kind of visceral continuity by the unfolding and deepening of their common orphic theme.

Four Years of Hate

It is not possible to open this essay on the cinematographic work of Jean Cocteau with a traditional biographical chapter; that story calls for an extraordinary book. "Jean Cocteau's masterpiece is his life," someone once remarked to Roger Lannes.[1] But to tell the story of Cocteau's life

[1] *Jean Cocteau*, by Roger Lannes, collection "Poètes d'aujourd'hui," Ed. Seghers.

would be to tell the story of his work, and conversely to write about the works of Jean Cocteau is to write about his life. In approaching this period of 1940–1944, in which the creator of *The Blood of a Poet* elects the cinema a second time and makes it his own, once for all, one cannot separate this act of choice and the artistic creation that ensues from Cocteau's personal existence. During these four years he was pursued by an indescribable eruption of hate, both from the collaborationist press and its columnists and from French fascist elements. In this climate of constant agitation and because of the exemplary strength of character that sustained Cocteau and infused his whole life, his creative activity swept along and ceaselessly intensified during these four trying years.

Where did Jean Cocteau stand at the opening of the war? After ten years of almost exclusive attention to the theatre and to journalism (for example, since 1937, and at the request of Louis Aragon, with whom he had become reconciled after the great surrealist quarrels, he contributed articles to the newspaper *Ce Soir*), Jean Cocteau had just come back to interior exploration, to a searching out of the mystery of poetry, in writing *La Fin du Potomak*. The first *Potomak* was written in 1913–1914, also just before the eruption of war. For the second time the poet turned his attention to this monstrous carrier of poetry, transmitter of poetry, with which he grappled, at the same time grappling with the world that surrounded and enclosed him. The "phony war" (1939–1940) found him in Paris, at the theatre: *Les Monstres sacrés* (The Holy Terrors), for Yvonne de Bray; as a curtain raiser, *Le Bel indifférent* for Edith Piaf. The campaign against Jean Cocteau was to begin with the revival of *Les Parents terribles,* in which Serge Reggiani replaced Jean Marais. It was a campaign of insults in the newspapers, and raids on the theatre by members of the Milice [1] and the P.P.F. [2] Incidents resumed with performances of *La Machine à ecrire* (*The Typewriter*) at the Théâtre Hébertot. First Fernand de Brinon, then the Germans, banned the play. The gravest difficulties with the German

---

[1] Milice—Occupation Militia.—Ed.
[2] P.P.F.—Parti Populaire Français, a French fascist party.—Ed.

and French authorities continued to plague Cocteau until the end of the Occupation.

For four years, Jean Cocteau was insulted tirelessly by a certain vermin, and by a political fringe in whose eyes he must have incarnated—more than others, who did not have this "dangerous visibility" [1]—individualism, humanism, and liberty. Jean Cocteau confronted insult, and rendered it nothingness by his activity: for *Comœdia* he wrote articles [2] in which he speaks of his beloved *monstres sacrés,* Yvonne de Bray, Marguerite Jamois, Arletty, and in which he pays homage to Giraudoux, Molière, Racine; he testified on behalf of Jean Genêt, reestablished his friendship with Paul Eluard, worked with Marcel Carné on a first adaptation (never to be produced) of *Juliette or the Key to Dreams (Juliette ou la clé des songes),* prefaced a Juliette Greco album. . . . And above all that, four new self-affirmations were his definitive reply to the forces that would have debased him. First, the beautiful return to written poetry, with the rhymed alexandrines of *Allégories,* as unexpected as they are finely wrought. Then his *Antigone* set to music by Arthur Honegger, which he himself directed at the Opéra, designing the sets and costumes as well. The invective of the press had no effect on the success of the play. And then *Renaud and Armide,* which the director of the Comédie-Française, Jean-Louis Vaudoyer, welcomed with intelligence and courage. Christian Bérard and Georges Auric supplied their collaboration in set design and music, and Jean Cocteau directed the production. In this play he revived dramatic verse, with magnificent "spoken arias," an opera of words. He had created a new and beautiful legend for these two legendary heroes, of whom he kept only the names, whereas for *The Eternal Return* he was to change only the names of the two heroes, and keep the myth intact. And with *The Eternal Return* we arrive at the fourth victory, his return to the cinema.

---

[1] Giraudoux said to him: "When they want to deal us a blow, they strike you. You are the ideal lightning rod to shield us from the bolt."

[2] Articles that he later collected under the title *Le Foyer des artistes,* along with the prewar articles published in *Ce Soir* ("Articles de Paris"). This collection was published in 1947.

Cocteau and the Filmmakers

The Phantom Baron (Serge de Poligny)
The Eternal Return (Jean Delannoy)
Les Dames du Bois de Boulogne (Robert Bresson)
La Voix humaine (Roberto Rossellini)
Ruy Blas (Pierre Billon)

A history of the French cinema will very likely remember a single film by the director Serge de Poligny: *The Phantom Baron;* of the filmmaker Pierre Billon, one film: *Ruy Blas;* and if a few titles will be remembered from the first phase of Jean Delannoy's career as having particularly contributed to the famous "tradition of quality" in French cinema of the 1940's, *The Eternal Return* is the one that will assuredly preserve the greatest portion of his prestige. These films owe something to Jean Cocteau, and he owes something to them. Cocteau said that he had learned much while working with Delannoy and that, at that time and under those conditions, he was obliged to learn. He, who twelve years earlier was quite capable of constructing cinematographically his autobiographical poem in language that captured the beauty of all primitive things, had understood with modesty that this poem was a unique work, a kind of fluke of technical unsophistication. He understood that fully to utilize "this incomparable vehicle of poetry," (the cinema) he would have to take other paths to attain the same end as *The Blood of a Poet,* and for a certain time to work beside professional craftsmen. There was of course another way—to sit through thirty showings of *The Rules of the Game,* or else through all of Murnau and all of Renoir: an unthinkable solution for a man like Cocteau. And then, too, he loved to mold things, and needed to follow the work of fine artisans. He prized this work, in its limits; he respected it. Cocteau followed the workings of the filmmaking machinery; he incorporated what he needed while leaving himself free to act according to his own interior mechanics. He did not exactly *learn* the craft; he merely ascertained that it was, in fact, his calling.

Cocteau contributed dialogue to *The Phantom Baron* of Serge de Poligny. The scenario, written by De Poligny, had been carved out and adapted in collaboration with Louis Chavance in the fall of 1942. Cocteau was interested in the film and above all in its atmosphere, which he defined this way: "Imagine an old château in ruins. A country house, an engagement banquet. Moats, lakes, swamps, dungeons, forests, and moonlight: that's *The Phantom Baron*." According to his view, the characters ought to identify themselves with these elements of décor and setting, and with these objects; living beings become themselves objects of mystery in this setting predestined for mystery, for unearthly adventure. But the fantastic that permeates the film is not, after all, its center. After the disappearance of Baron Carol, the crumbling old château is succeeded by a manor house inhabited by the baron's descendants. The story Jean Cocteau was to unfold is a drama of the heart's first awakenings and uncertainties. Thus he had the happy fortune to meet characters who were waiting for him to endow them with their psychological and dramatic outlines.

In 1943, Cocteau took another step forward with a work in which he was more profoundly engaged: *The Eternal Return*. Not only did he write the scenario and the dialogue; he also brought with him Jean Marais, Yvonne de Bray, and another member of the "tribe," Georges Auric. He reestablished acquaintance with the director of photography, Roger Hubert, who had also been photography director for *The Phantom Baron*. For Cocteau, this film was not merely a question of an adaptation-transposition, with which he already had had several experiences (*Oedipus Rex; Antigone,* based on Sophocles; with even more creative license, but still rooted in Greek myth, *The Infernal Machine;* based on medieval mythology, *Knights of the Round Table*). It was rather a question of bringing close to us, more vividly this time, the courtly legend, the "romance" of Tristan and Yseult. In the literary reworking of the legend that Joseph Bédier wrote by adapting the original sources, Bédier led us back toward the medieval work, brought us closer to it. On the other hand, Richard Wagner, in his lyric drama, cultivated the unfamiliar and spiritual medievality, in contrast to the modernity of his musical creation. Jean Cocteau chose to transport the theme and the force lines of the courtly romance right into the twentieth century, based on the same dramatic and affective givens, the repetition of the same emotional and dramatic developments.

If one excepts his first play, *Romeo and Juliet,* for which he did not have to construct the drama, and *The Human Voice,* for which a structured drama was unnecessary, Jean Cocteau had already experienced, by the time he wrote *The Eternal Return,* eight very diverse instances of the "poetry of theatre" as he called it, of dramatic elaboration. Strong in his craft from this experience, and with great mastery and accomplishment, he wrote his modern Tristan and Yseult (renaming the characters Patrice and Nathalie), giving it a title borrowed from Nietzsche. The medium of cinema would have permitted him an epic reconstruction of the story, epic and "poetic" in the anti-Cocteau sense of the word: highly painted. It would have permitted him, even in a modern transposition, to keep the profusion of narrative developments, the vicissitudes, the parade of kings and barons and monsters. Cocteau, however, chose to compress the elements that led him from courtly romance to tragedy, and he wove the action from a single gold thread, a single golden hair from Yseult the Blonde. Tristan's baron enemies, for example, become a single family whose hate and attendant perfidies find an even more violently poisonous crucible; and tragic realism gains. On a higher plane, however, the three characters disengage themselves from the temporal; they have only first names, and they love each other in the eternal present. But where to place Achille, unique and omnipotent propeller of all action, source and end of the tragedy, Achille who opens and closes the film by killing? On the plane of the gods then. "The gods do exist," wrote Cocteau somewhere; "they are the devil." The Frossin family hates Tristan with a bitter hatred, but only Achille the dwarf—the burning center of the family as well as the concentrated center of its hatred—is moved to action. Achille is fate, evil, the gods forever jealous of man, gods over which man can triumph only in death. And it is against Achille that the love of Tristan and Yseult—Patrice and Nathalie— triumphs in death. Theme of impossible love? Perhaps, but it's not quite that simple, for we are dealing here with a tragic theme. With all the diversities of nuance and situation, it is the theme of *The Infernal Machine* as well as the theme of *Les Enfants terribles* and *Renaud et Armide;* but it is also the situation of Sophie-Yvonne de Bray in *Les Parents terribles;* it is the "death" of Orpheus. One dies of loving. This is not exactly an impossible love, but rather such a total, exalted, redemptive love that it can exist and be consummated only as it advances inexorably toward death, toward the great, tragic dénouement.

One begins to understand why Jean Cocteau chose this celebrated tale and why he was not tempted to modify and remodel the dramatic continuity of the legend after his own fashion. At the very most he contributes a subtle and opportune shift in the episode of the philter. Marie-Anne, who raised Nathalie, prepared for the young girl the herb wine that was intended to bind her to a husband many years her senior. Patrice and Nathalie drink the liquid that Achille has poured into their wine as poison. Their mood approaches intoxication, but it is also an intoxication of the heart, for they have already sensed love aborning between them. Jean Cocteau has thus retained the device of the philter, but the mystery goes beyond this simple artifice. Cocteau acts, according to his rule and his personal formula, as the organizer behind it all: poison—false poison, love potion useless in a love already born, beverage absorbed in double inutility, double sense of the intoxication of Patrice and Nathalie, and twofold significance of Nathalie's exclamation at the end of the storm that accompanies this whole scene, "We've had a narrow escape." What does she think they have escaped? From what does she so fearfully desire to escape? This relationship between the drinking of the potion and the birth of passion is an example of the "accidental synchronization" dear to Cocteau. That is, in Cocteau's version the potion does not *cause* the passion, but is, by accident, synchronous with it. This question of "accidental synchronization" will be discussed in more detail later.

In any case, here we have one of the most remarkable instances of inventiveness in this modern re-creation of Tristan and Yseult. Another, on a totally different plane, is the violent incarnation of all Tristan's enemies in the single personage of Achille, heir no doubt of the dwarf

The Eternal Return: **Roland Toutain, Junie Astor, Jean Marais.** *Discina*

Frocin [1], but surpassing the latter in all the malevolent forces Cocteau accumulates and concentrates in him.

In *The Eternal Return*, Jean Cocteau confronts a moral and poetic universe that he acknowledged as his own. He neither adopts nor adapts it, but enters it easily, and sets sail upon it. Perhaps he needed to travel in an elsewhere that sufficiently resembled his own world, before reopening this world at the heart of his films. During an entire episode of *The Eternal*

[1] The dwarf Frocin is a malevolent figure in the original Tristan legend. The Frossin family derives its name from Frocin (in French, Frossin and Frocin would be pronounced the same way), and the dwarf Achille is obviously the direct incarnation of the dwarf Frocin.—ED.

Return we are reminded of the singular existence of his personal world and its familiar mythology; it is the scene in the garage where Lionel lives with his sister in a climate somewhat "enfants terribles" and somewhat "gipsy caravan." This is the scene that was most often questioned as a suspicious break in the tone of the film. Roger Régent called it "an interlude among the monkey wrenches and carburetor breakdowns," after which the authors come back to "their happy formulas of the beginning." Jean Cocteau himself protested this error in his chapter "Of the Marvelous in Cinematography," in *The Difficulty of Being:* "In *The Eternal Return,* the lovers' château seems to our critics to be appropriate to poetry, and the garage of the brother and sister inappropriate. They condemn it. What strange nonsense. For it is precisely in this garage that poetry functions best. In effect, better to understand the abandon of the brother and sister, their innate and somehow organic ignorance of grace, one prods it with a finger, and I approach the terrible mysteries of love."

Attacks of another sort were later made on this film, notably on the part of English critics who, in 1946, accused Cocteau of having "Germanized" *Tristan and Yseult.*

To which Cocteau replied: "Epochs dominated by politics (partisan epochs) are inappropriate to criticism. Critical opinion during the Occupation decided in advance that I was ignoble, and ignoble were my undertakings. English critics in 1946 accuse *The Eternal Return,* a Welsh legend, of being of German inspiration because the hero and heroine are blond (*sic*)."

Cocteau wished to be, and was, a free man; so naturally he was attacked unsparingly from all sides. Soon enough, *Beauty and the Beast* suffered its share of irrelevant criticism. In France, it was sacrificed on the altar of neorealist confusions and the mystifications of self-styled "committed" art.

1944: Jean Cocteau finished a long poem, *Léone,* the birth of a new mythical creature, a new angel, whom we must keep in mind when we turn our attention to *The Blood of a Poet* and to its offspring, *Orpheus* and *Testament of Orpheus.* On July 6, 1944, Cocteau was dealt a new blow; once again friendship was violently torn from him. Jean Desbordes—whom

Cocteau had discovered and supported (as he had Raymond Radiguet), by committing himself in 1928, in the preface of his book *J'adore,* to Desbordes, to whom he said: ". . . You are a little brother to Antigone. The smallest word from you offends the city"—died the day after his arrest, in Gestapo headquarters.

For that whole year, Cocteau's name was associated with the enormous success of *The Eternal Return*: he was credited, in the restrictive sense one gave the expression at that time, as author of the film, which is to say as scriptwriter. But Jean Cocteau could never be a script-dialogue writer in the same sense as a Charles Spaak or an Henri Jeanson. *The Eternal Return* is an epiphany, the first signs (excepting *The Blood of a Poet,* which was made on the periphery of the cinema), the first stars of Cocteau's poetic universe to appear on the public screen. One sensed that this could herald a return, a rebirth of the poet into cinema. Cocteau was himself aware of the extent of his contribution to a film that, still and all, was a film of Jean Delannoy, marked in its pace and rhythm, in the direction of its actors, by the manner and conception of Delannoy.

Cocteau began to dream of *Beauty and the Beast.* He was already working on it when, out of friendship for Robert Bresson, he agreed to write the dialogues for *Les Dames du Bois de Boulogne,* while Marais refused the role of Jean in Bresson's film because he was preparing for his role as the Beast. The producer, Raoul Ploquin, rejoiced: "I'm going to have Bresson plus some Cocteau!" It was precisely that: an addition. It couldn't have been otherwise. Neither Cocteau nor Bresson would have wanted it otherwise. Cocteau chose to place himself outside all possible disagreement with Bresson; he accepted discipline; Bresson gave him the scenes and the number of lines. Cocteau was asked for words, and he produced them, with aloofness and distinction, with intelligence and with rather little personal involvement. Nevertheless there runs through this text—a stylistic exercise— a certain muffled sensibility that is not at all Bresson and that has, oddly enough, echoes of Diderot. The curious part of the business was that Cocteau most certainly took his tone from Diderot, with whom, however, he refused to admit the slightest affinity. He molded a dialogue: There was a tone to be found, an elegance, a measure, a certain quality of preciousness, a major preciousness—in short, domineering language—for characters that Cocteau had neither chosen nor created. It was obvious that it did not displease him to make them speak.

Once he had finished working with Robert Bresson and *Les Dames du Bois de Boulogne,* Cocteau again took up the task of preparing *Beauty and the Beast,* and from August through December, 1945, he shot his film. In January, 1946, the film premiered in Paris; in December it received the Louis Delluc prize. The year 1946 was one of pause for the new filmmaker. Twice he returned to the stage, for the creation of his ballet-mime-drama, *Le Jeune Homme et la Mort* (Death and the Young Man), at the Théâtre des Champs-Elyseés, and for the production of *L'Aigle à deux têtes,* played by Edwige Feuillère and Jean Marais. It was a year of written poetry as well, with the publication of *La Crucifixion.* A rich year—but what year in the life of Jean Cocteau hadn't been rich, since 1909 when he published his first poems, *La Lampe d'Aladin?* The work of this year had its effect on Cocteau's cinema, not only because *L'Aigle à deux têtes* was to become a film in 1947, with the same actors, but also because the idea of "accidental synchronization" occurred to Cocteau and was first deliberately used by him during the creation of *Le Jeune Homme et la Mort.* In this ballet spectacle, Roland Petit's choreography (Jean Babilée was the young man) had been structured on jazz rhythms, whereas it was, in effective incongruity, performed to the Passacaglia of J. S. Bach. Dance and music precipitated one another, in the implacable synchronization of this directed accident. Cocteau transposed this idea of controlled gratuitousness to his films, in their scoring, and in the relationship of text to image. He fled from imposing any "poetic" effects on an organically simple structure; rather, the text becomes simple and naked because the image is already poetry. As early as *The Blood of a Poet* Cocteau had shifted certain passages of Georges Auric's music, juxtaposing them haphazardly with images other than those for which they had been composed. With more complexity and subtlety, these accidents were organized anew in *Orpheus.*

The years 1947 and 1948 were essentially cinematographic for Cocteau. In May, 1947, he flanked Roberto Rossellini during the shooting of *La Voix humaine;* shortly afterward he assisted Pierre Billon while Billon directed *Ruy Blas;* in October he produced his own *L'Aigle à deux têtes* at the château de Vizille; in February, 1948, *Ruy Blas* opened in Paris, and *L'Aigle* in September. Meanwhile, Cocteau had completed *Les Parents terribles,* which came out in November. There was just time left to sketch the design for a tapestry, "Judith and Holophernes," [1] and at the end of December he took off for America, writing his famous *Lettre aux Américains* on the return flight.

He had watched Rossellini shoot his film. "I entrusted *La Voix humaine* to Roberto Rossellini because he is supple and is not encumbered by any of those dead restrictions that rule the cinema." Cocteau knew from experience that this scorn for rules had its dangers, but the risk was good and fruitful. He described *Paisan* as "a masterpiece in which a people expressed itself through a man and a man through a people." For him Rossellini portrayed himself and told his own story while painting the portrait of a bruised and suffering Italy by recounting episodically several moments in the life of the Italy of 1944, just as the author of *The Blood of a Poet* drew his own portrait by capturing in four episodes several moments in the life of a poet. Jean Cocteau was never detached, indifferent to the history of his time. During the shooting of *Beauty and the Beast,* to give only one instance, Cocteau was obsessed by the Nuremberg trials. But it fell to Rossellini to make *Paisan* as it would fall to other filmmakers to film other *Paisan*s which they could not help making. Cocteau loved these films if they were good films (too many *engagé* works had nothing to recommend them except titles like *Vivre en paix*), but for himself he had to return to his myths and his poetry, to continue to create out of time. Every epoch has need of its fables and poets. But a large number of French critics—misunderstanding the nature of neorealism and under the spell of cinema as a "witness to its time"—condemned Cocteau's films in the name of *Rome, Open City,* and *Paisan* (and *Les Enfants du Paradis* as well!)

The same "committed" group sulked over *Ruy Blas* either in the name

---

[1] The tapestry can be seen in *Testament of Orpheus.* A little girl, questioned by Henry Torrès, stands before it answering questions as if she were on a television quiz show.

Jean Marais in *Ruy Blas*.

of meaningful cinema or in the name of Victor Hugo! [1] Jean Cocteau did indeed rewrite *Ruy Blas*—and it was well he did so! He recomposed and structured more rigorously than Hugo, distilling the substance of the dialogue from the Alexandrines, melting the work down by washing away, with the acid precision of his language, the expletives, the surplus words, the monotonously purring rhythms. He wrote as "active a film as possible," as he called it, that is, an action film, in the best "movie" sense of the term, but also a film of actions, that is, a film of acts, as one may call his theatre a theatre of acts. Cocteau himself has used the term Western in reference to this film; he was wrong, to be sure, but at least he put it orally in quotes. This *Ruy Blas* is an adventure film, a cloak-and-dagger movie, the first and finest of those later filmed, in the same genre, with Jean Marais. "I didn't commit my substance [to this film], because it was more a game than an internal necessity. It's for this reason that I entrusted it to a director

1 The film *Ruy Blas* was adapted from Victor Hugo's long poem of the same name.—ED.

[Pierre Billon] whom I assisted to some extent, and whose rhythm I could not possibly have altered." Still, one senses the pleasure Cocteau derived from writing this film and from participating in its production. If Victor Hugo could boast of having broken and disjointed this great simpleton, the Alexandrine, Cocteau was able, in his turn, to wield a wholesome scythe in the Alexandrine underbrush of the Hugolian *Ruy Blas.* That is why it is particularly interesting to read this adaptation, to follow the work of this excellent gardener, and to consider his sense of measure, equilibrium, proportion, and his taste for efficient simplicity.

Of Bicephalousness

L'Aigle à deux têtes
(*The Two-Headed Eagle*)

Oddly enough, *L'Aigle à deux têtes* is the unknown, forgotten film of Jean Cocteau. I have often caught accomplished cinephiles in such flagrant forgetfulness, even while they hail *Ruy Blas,* and this ignorance extends even to film clubs. This neglect can be traced back to the reception accorded the film when it first appeared near the end of 1947. It was well received, of course, but not as it ought to have been. The film was very much out of the fashionable mainstream. The splendor of *Beauty and the Beast* succeeded in making what some felt to be an anachronism quite palatable. *Ruy Blas* had benefited from Jean Marais, the briskness of an adventure film, the evocations of a Grade-B movie. But this time, in the context of cinema 1948, the choice of this particular story, and of this atmosphere, was almost an act of provocation in the eyes of those who were inclined to class Cocteau among the cursed ranks of bourgeois and decadently uncommitted artists, those artists who turned their backs to the realities of their own time, as the saying went. As if the most profound expression of the realities of any particular time were not often to be found in the enactment of the realities of all time. In any event, such was the path chosen by Jean Cocteau, this voyager in space-time, familiar com-

panion of the eternal myths. Who, in 1947, would have dared to speak of the realism of Jean Cocteau—even if he had been aware of it? Nevertheless, the author of *L'Aigle à deux têtes* remained loyal to his own sense of tragic realism, once again aided in this truth by Christian Bérard.[1]

Was it the movie version of *Ruy Blas* that inspired Jean Cocteau to make a film version of his play *L'Aigle à deux têtes* as well? Or was it the play that prompted him to write a film adaptation of *Ruy Blas*? *L'Aigle* dates from 1945–1946, and at any rate it is a much more significant work than *Ruy Blas*. Edwige Feuillère and Jean Marais starred in *L'Aigle* at the Théâtre Hébertot. The film that Cocteau drew from the play in 1947 was thoroughly readapted for the new medium; the screenplay was substantially rewritten from the play's text, adapted into a form that opens the work wide from the physical constrictions of the play. (A similar opening process occurred in transposing *Ruy Blas* and *Les Parents terribles*—both of which had only two sets in their stage versions—from the stage to film.) Through the medium of film, *L'Aigle* bursts into space, into the exterior world, calling upon the riches of Bérard and of the landscape itself, as if it wished to translate the profound aspirations and the enthrallments of this romantic queen. This opening out also counterbalances the closed, rigid, alien world of the court. Here Jean Cocteau chose to lead us rather than rivet us to a certain viewpoint; he induces us to follow along and discover the queen revealed in a simple truth of absolute inconformity to the traditional popular and theatrical conception of a queen.

The dramatic structure is not greatly altered, retaining what one might call its Mozartian musical lines: First movement, the queen's theme and

[1] Christian Bérard was Cocteau's set director and/or costume director for *Beauty and the Beast, L'Aigle à deux têtes, Les Parents terribles,* and he had roughed out the work for *Orpheus* when he died. His extraordinary rapport with Cocteau allowed him to serve as the perfect instrument for the concrete expression of Cocteau's ideas on establishing atmosphere and tone through décor and costume design.—ED.

L'Aigle à deux têtes: Sylvia Monfort, Edwige Feuillère, and Jean Debucourt. Sirius

variations; second movement, Stanislas' theme; third movement, in two parallel lines, the Comte de Foehn and the queen, and the Comte and Stanislas; fourth movement, the tragic finale. Two persons meet, unite, after having first clashed, and sacrifice themselves one to the other and to the unit of themselves. Since the death of the king, the queen has sought to give tragic form to her life; she forces tragedy, struggles against a destiny that threatens banality and compels it to become tragic at the price of a last scene in which she forces herself to play to Stanislas. Theatricality is no longer in the theatre, but in the queen herself. The queen provokes a tragic death and the fulfillment of fatality—in contrast, say, to Orpheus, who accepts such a death but does not seek it out; she obstinately constructs an unlooked-for grandness and destiny on the cornerstone of an exceptional encounter in which chance, momentarily deflected from its path, rights itself in perfect orientation on another plane. A political assassination transforms itself into a crime of passion, a murder of love and wounded pride, whereas the man who strikes the blow is already prey to the death that seeps through his veins, and the stricken woman has ferociously extracted and conquered this death-dealing blow by means of a deliberately provocative lie of which she is able to absolve herself as she confronts the death she has provoked. In this encounter, the queen discovered a means of outwitting a destiny whose first proposition she is thus able to refuse. In the same encounter the anarchist poet, the *carbonaro,* discovers the possibility of transcending the absurdly narrow limits of an individual act of terrorism, of going beyond his methodical and rational nineteenth-century nihilism, philosophy that smacks more of Hegel than of Nietzsche and is consequently devoid of lyricism. Nevertheless, Cocteau does not allow Stanislas to fall into the snare of passion; his suicide is not in the least passional, but, rather, philosophical. It is a sacrifice: voluntarily surrendering up the queen to an image of herself that he does not wish to impair. Thus, *L'Aigle à deux têtes,* a far greater play than *Ruy Blas,* becomes a superior film as well. The honest respect that Jean Cocteau manifested for Victor Hugo in *Ruy Blas* is evident in the fact that he did not wish to give the appearance of enlarging upon Hugo's own efforts. Within the changed form, Cocteau retained Hugo's spirit, manner, and genre: he made an adventure film. Why elevate the subject of *Ruy Blas*? In contrast, *L'Aigle à deux têtes* yields much more than a story of sudden passion and of resemblances. (Jean Cocteau was obviously fond of the resemblance theme, although no serious consequence ever derived from it; it was one of his insignia, a figure on his coat of arms.)

L'Aigle—a majestic, formal, even stern work—is a moral and political tragedy. The point of departure was marked by historical analogies—the story of Elisabeth of Austria, assassinated by a madman, had already inspired Barrès—but Cocteau did not choose to write a historical drama. Although the point of departure was exceptionally romantic, Cocteau did an immediate about-face and concentrated exclusively on the tragic aspect, avoiding his usual mixture of tones. The film is marked by nobility, grandeur, even majesty, in their naked truth, which is to say undistorted by heavy-laden solemnity and quickened by human warmth. At the same time, Cocteau protects the myriad nuances of the characters' intimate authenticity. It is not through words that grandeur is achieved. Certainly the language is very beautiful and of high quality, but it is of difficult simplicity; unencumbered by a single ornament, it neither weighs upon the characters nor does it dominate them. Language does not "make" the characters any more than the drama precedes or creates them. For Cocteau, it is always the characters themselves who secrete the structure of the drama and of its language. Thus the actors are all the more rigorously chained to the personages they interpret, and Jean Cocteau is the most tenderly attentive and infallible of jailers. He never left Edwige Feuillère the opportunity to take herself seriously; he is the one who takes her seriously, which is more important. Cocteau leads her into becoming the captive of her character rather than allowing her to capture the character in the nets of professional tricks and habits, even those of such a great actress. Sylvia Monfort, stranger and more disquieting than ever, because she plays with more simplicity, is Edith de Berg. She alone might have been able to replace Maria Casarès in the role of the Princess in *Orpheus*. It was impossible that Jean Cocteau should not work with her at least once more.[1]

---

[1] She later played in a television production of *La Machine infernale* (1963).

Jean Marais, who was at the same time demonstrating in *Les Parents terribles* that he is one of those rare and exceptional actors who knows how to suffer and to cry, shows in *L'Aigle à deux têtes* that he is capable, on both stage and screen, of doing two terribly difficult things: of exulting with all his soul and all his physical being, and of dying a great and tragic death.

Shadows of Two Mavericks

Les Enfants terribles
(Jean-Pierre Melville)

"I think *Les Enfants terribles* is an exceptional venture. I had always refused requests. I accepted Melville's because his maverick style seemed to me apt to communicate to this film the improvisational allure of the sixteen-millimeter film I've spoken to you about. . . ." This was Jean Cocteau's reply to André Fraigneau in *Entretiens autour du cinématographe*,[1] although he didn't explain why he hadn't decided himself to direct this new rendering of his novel, and Fraigneau, unfortunately, didn't think to ask him the question. In any case, in the French film world of 1950, Cocteau and Melville were certainly—and Cocteau would remain so to the end—mavericks, maverick partisans of cinema. It's a curious combination, nonetheless; for although they both resisted a common enemy—the commercial, or rather the professional, world of filmmakers, the corporation with all its pomp and production, its usages, rites, laws, interdictions, timidity, its trade unions and rules, in sum its habits good and bad—they hardly belonged to the same esthetic family, or even to the same family of men. Yet here they are, both engaged in the same enterprise, making a low-budget, freehanded film. While Jean Cocteau wrote the adaptation and dialogue, Jean-Pierre Melville presided as producer over a modest film, without a single star. Cocteau followed the production

[1] Editions André Bonne.

L'Aigle à deux têtes: **Jean Marais.**

closely, and during a period when Melville was ill, he filmed a summer seaside scene (although it was, in fact, the middle of winter) at Montmorency by himself. The decision—actually a result of financial necessity—to film on location, and the choice of film sites, pleased him: Melville's apartment (which the latter had rented only in the hope of using it in the film), the hall of *Le Petit Journal*, "whose hideousness could never be duplicated," said Cocteau; the "Laurent" restaurant, and the Théâtre Pigalle, transformed into a poor man's film studio, whose movable stage served in lieu of a dolly, which they couldn't afford.

We're dealing here with the adaptation of a novel to the screen; a familiar enough occurrence. This one, however, was lucky enough to escape tradition, to be a completely new departure.

In point of fact, the passage of this novel into film occurred through complete metamorphosis, and not simply through a change in metabolism; Cocteau sought to give the work a second birth, as changed through the medium of cinema. He conserved scenes from the novel with existing dialogues, and created especially for the film other scenes dictated by the structure of the novel. For these new scenes he wrote new dialogues in the style of the novel. And finally, he selected several passages from the novel to read himself, incorporated as narration into the film—a device he absolutely refused to use in his own films, in which, on the contrary, the text is always extremely sober and stripped of all verbal poetry, in order to avoid overloading, and thereby abusing the poetry born of the images themselves. Nevertheless, in *Les Enfants terribles,* this interpolation of the verbal is present; it contributes something to the film—exactly the same thing furnished by the passages from the novel *Jules and Jim* in François Truffaut's film: the echo of another form of poetry, of another kind of beauty, a few beams from another source of light falling upon the characters, the accompaniment of a still-spoken music.

But the pure musical accompaniment in *Les Enfants terribles* also deviates from the tradition set by Cocteau in his own films. Georges Auric is missing here, and, to accompany this film drawn from an analytical novel—and the film consciously cultivated that analytical aspect—Melville chose classical music. He selected a Vivaldi concerto for four violins and orchestra, transcribed by J. S. Bach for four pianos and orchestra, and a concerto grosso in A minor. Cocteau used this approach only for his danced mime-drama, *Le Jeune Homme et la Mort,* in an effort to provoke the sort of accidental synchronization discussed earlier. This "accident" occurs in *Les Enfants terribles* as well, for the music—as often happens when classical music is stripped of all descriptive, narrative, or symbolist intentions, and of all voluntary dramatic expression—this abstract music becomes the most figurative of feeling, of passion and drama, and yet retains the free and unalterable brilliancy of its harmonic structure. In the context of the film this inspired chamber music expresses extraordinarily well the spirit of the chamber—this room crammed with objects, an abstract setting capable of re-creating itself anywhere, and at the heart of which presides Elisabeth, the god-figure.

Collaborations and harmonies were somewhat less happy with respect to the acting, which suffered imbalances never present in Cocteau's own work and which never again appear in Melville's. Cocteau lamented Melville's insistence on having Renée Cosima play both Dargelos and Agathe: "Dargelos is such a male character, possessed of a prestige which could only belong to a youth in the pride of his manly prerogatives, that even the most talented of actresses would be implausible in the role."

If Edouard Dermit, in *Orpheus* and in *Testament of Orpheus,* is often touching in his sincerity, in his vaguely gauche strength, and in the very fact that he lacks the presence of an actor and that Cocteau knew how to capitalize on this absence and on the absent airs of the poet Cégeste, a soul in no-man's-land, Dermit unfortunately, in *Les Enfants terribles,* develops an excess of theatrical presence that is decidedly out of place. His strength, even though gauche, is not inappropriate to Cégeste, but it is completely foreign to Paul's physical and moral fragility. Nevertheless, Edouard Dermit has a few marvelous moments when he is literally carried away by the diabolical game of Nicole Stéphane. How she must have fascinated and exhilarated Jean Cocteau, who was present at the filming— a more enthralled spectator than any first-night audience! She is entirely consumed by impetuosity and passionate impulses, by tenderness, violence, and contradictions, tyrannical purity and possessive, lying maneuvers. She ravages all our skepticisms, our tepidities, forcing us to enter the procession of infuriatingly theatrical scenes that make up Elisabeth's life. Then suddenly there is the sweetness, the appeasement of a simple moment in which Nicole Stéphane discovers new treasures, new gestures and expressions, a mobility of hands and face that are part and parcel of the room's "treasure" and without which the treasure itself would be merely a hodgepodge of objects without personal value, empty of life or poetry. In *Les Enfants terribles,* Nicole Stéphane was a very young and very great actress, as was Nicole Berger in *Le Blé en herbe* at exactly the same period. Need one be reminded that French cinema first ignored and then forgot them both?

Les Enfants terribles was truly an unexpected film, or rather, one didn't know from whom to expect it: from the author of the novel or from Melville, the director of *Silence de la Mer*. The director of photography was Henri Decaë, another maverick and a hard photographer in every sense of the term, with a hard image-style that suited both Cocteau (it is the same style which he demanded from Henri Alekan in *Beauty and the Beast*) and Melville. But the latter alone is responsible for the flickering, mordant tone of the film; American in the classic tradition, it is very close to the style that was soon to become Melville's signature, and very far from the Doric harmonies of Cocteau's own work. A strange film, certainly a film that engages something deep, it is beautiful and haunting like Cocteau, prehensible and incisive like Melville; and yet nothing seems less like either a Cocteau film or a film by Melville than this one. Had Cocteau perhaps sensed that for him this work, among all his literary works, must remain a novel and that he would not be able to submit it to his own cinematographic form? In any case, he left the work to Melville, and he loved Melville's film.

Mythologie française   *Beauty and the Beast*

The year was 1945, in the moribund month of August. "In Touraine the Loire flowed, flat, beneath a sky of pale sun." Jean Cocteau, Christian Bérard, Henri Alekan, Jean Marais, Josette Day, Mila Parély, Nane Germon, Michel Auclair, and "the group" so dear to "the general," as his crew called him, a whole crowd of traveling bohemians gathered in the manor house of Rochecorbon in Ille-et-Vilaine. Cocteau had discovered this country house by happy accident, in one of those conjunctions of need and the answer to need that constantly occur in life, though people are reluctant to accept them in fiction. But this was indeed an enchantment: Cocteau *recognized* down to the smallest detail the setting for Beauty's house that he had feared he would have to build from scratch; even the iron grillwork of the manor represented a fabulous beast. "Everything is in its place," he wrote in his film diary. "The interior corresponds to the exterior, and this secret exactitude radiates across the ramparts. We have only to move the sun—that is, to move ourselves several times during each scene according to the sun's course."

August, 1945. Jean Cocteau directs the first scenes of the first film for which he has assumed entire responsibility since *The Blood of a Poet,* and from the outset this film labors under the sign of ordeal and struggle: against illness, against injuries that assail them all wickedly—Cocteau, Jean Marais, Mila Parély—against material difficulties, and against the capricious sky of Touraine. The film is also made under the sign of anachronism and countercurrents. At Rochecorbon they await the arrival of René Clément, who is to supply technical assistance. In Brittany, Clément still has to finish the final takes on *La Bataille du rail,* the famous scene of the armored train's derailment by sabotage. (Cocteau was passionately enthusiastic about Clément's film: "An admirable film," he said, "played by trainmen and locomotives.")

The story of *Beauty and the Beast* is from the fairy tale by Mme. Leprince de Beaumont—the story but not the poetry of its filmic retelling. Cocteau's point of departure was the fairy tale and its moral, or rather its morality, in which the marvelous is simply one of the givens: clear, traditional, necessary—a means. The fact of the fabulous, then, is never an end in itself. Certainly, we begin in the universe of the fairy tale, the realm of fairies and of the lesson to be learned. The fairies are present. But Cocteau evicts the fairies, and once again sets out to track down "the realism of the irreal." He tightens the dramatic structure and strips the denouement of its traditional trappings in which the family, the prince, and his subjects are reunited by a wave of the good fairy's magic wand. In contrast, he invents the character of Avenant who dies that the Beast might be reborn through him and in his image, and devises a very simple finale in which Prince Ardent and Beauty take wing, as in The Thousand and One Nights, toward a kingdom that we shall not see. In fact, all Cocteau's work whispers to us of this kingdom where neither day nor night, good nor evil, truth nor falsehood, nor time will exist, and where his characters find each other again at the end of his stories—whatever might be the clarity or obscurity, the substance or the lack of substance with which he endows that beyond.

With *Beauty and the Beast* Jean Cocteau neared the completion of his cycle of medieval French mythology: *Les Chevaliers de la Table Ronde, Renaud et Armide, L'Eternel Retour.* Actually, Western mythology would be a more appropriate term, since the origins of Tristan and Yseult are Welsh and Danish, as well as Norman and German—French in the final analysis, but in the medieval sense of the term. The final contribution to this cycle was his ballet *La Dame à la licorne,* first performed in Munich in 1953 and again at the Paris Opéra in 1959.

The theme that rests at the heart of Cocteau's work is the theme posited most clearly in *Orpheus*: the choice between love and poetry. And it is clear, if one takes the world of the Beast as the world of exceptions and of poetry, and the face of the handsome prince as the countenance of love, that the great Orphic theme animates *Beauty and the Beast* as well. It has absolutely nothing to do with the idea of love judged and rejected. Love is simply *said*, a difficult and indeed formidable task, for the demands of the muse are most exclusive.

In all his works Cocteau had the opportunity to exploit a popular theme, to elaborate, utilize, deploy, and orchestrate. He always did the contrary: he tightened, reinvented, and bound his work in the tightest and most violent cords of tragedy—and did this so well that everything always harks back in some measure to *La Machine infernale,* both in Greek overtones and in the sense that Cocteau occidentalized with metaphysical anxiety everything he drew from the Greek myths. Hence he takes his place in the ancient chain of mythic continuity that links Leda to King Kong and passes through all the Dianas of hart and hare—this splendid Beauty and Beast of the château of Anet!—and through *La Dame à la licorne.*[1] But, as always, once the roots of a work have been firmly established,

---

[1] A tale of a Belle Dame in love with the Unicorn Beast. She cannot love the handsome knight except at the cost of the Unicorn's life. So again the choice is posited between poetry and love.—ED.

Cocteau's version undergoes its customary tropisms, pushing its tendrils and efflorescence toward an Orphic light. Beauty and the Beast have become characters of Jean Cocteau's dramaturgy even if the story here diverges from the structures of drama, turning instead to a rhythmic portrayal of the narrative form. It is a fairy tale, in the form of "once upon a time," and Cocteau narrates the tale admirably, in supremely pure, cinematographic language. There is not a single instance of commentary, of recitative, but rather a cinematic narrative, continuous, fluid, with a splendid and noble rhythm, with adagios that paradoxically take off from short, rapid scenes—like all those that take place in Beauty's house. An even more difficult accomplishment: *Beauty and the Beast* is a film of acts, therefore a film of action, morally and formally, whereas the original fairy tale offers no gradations or angles, nothing to grasp. The context is still a fairy tale, but if Jean Cocteau appeals to the soul of our childhood, it is to capture our confidence better; he asks us to believe, before and rather than admiring, for he knew he had again denied the public—had done it the honor of refusing to offer—all the sentimental and formal complicities that one might expect from such a film: no ostentatious emotions, only secret ones, no appeal to pity or sentimentality or terror, or to puerile and virtuous morality, no merely spectacular or eye-catching evocation of the fantastic. Everything proceeds necessarily from the language and the story, told simply and well, and the beauty and poetry spring forth in radiant and spontaneous joy from this justice and simplicity, this bold, luminous, infallible measure and tact.

Beast, Beauty. The Beast of Mme. Leprince de Beaumont did not exist; according to the story, one doesn't see him—in fact, one doesn't *see* anything, for the story is the abstraction, or rather the nonfiguration, nonrepresentation, of beings and objects. Cocteau created the Beast, morally, conceived him, gave him life—indeed, gave him a soul; Christian Bérard clothed the Beast, gave him a mask, actually a face; Jean Marais incarnated the Beast, which is to say lent him—indeed, literally gave him his own flesh. Consequently, I must take exception to the term "monster" currently used with reference to the Beast. For a certain period of time he is both the momentary incarnation of a being and a being in and of himself, and

thus bears a double risk: the risk that this period of time might be a life-time, and the risk of a death without salvation, of death without recall, of a life without transcendence of self, without renascence through love. The Beast is dominated above all by waiting and by anxiety for a deliverance and a conquest of self that he cannot accomplish except through the conquest of another being. Jean Cocteau endowed his character with a portion of feline bestiality: his ears perk and quiver at the passage of a doe, and he laps water from a pool—details quite as important as the fur, the long sharp teeth, and the murderous claws. But this bestiality is that of a thoroughbred, not of brutality or savagery. We soon come to love the Beast, as his creator loved him, and as he will make him beloved by Beauty. Thus, the Beast is removed from the monster of mythology; certainly we recall, though hazily and only afterward, that Zeus descended to earth seeking pleasure in the form of a bull, but the god neither expected nor hoped for love from the beautiful mortal; he simply raped her. The god was neither good nor generous nor loyal; the gods are not good; they are violent and egocentric. The Beast waits and wants to be loved, as he must; for the Beast is condemned to make himself loved. He seeks love through his goodness, generosity, and loyalty, whereas out of Beauty's presence, he is bloodthirsty and violent. Yet, when Beauty feels the first stirrings of emotion, her first tentative affection for the Beast, it is aroused not by all these good qualities, but by an unexpected and moving manifestation of his animality. The Beast, stretched out on the ground, is lapping water from the pool, and Beauty is suddenly moved to offer him a drink from her cupped hands; for the first time the tongue and lips and fleece of the Beast's face touch Beauty's skin. Is it necessary to point out that all this is not in the written story? At another time, when the Beast returns from the hunt, chest heaving, steamy, and covered with blood, Beauty feels more reprobation than horror. Soon Beauty is saying "my Beast" with tenderness, almost as a mistress says *mon chat* to her lover. But the demands and gestures of the Beast are indeed those of a lover. For example, the Beast's desire to watch Beauty as she dines is told, surely with naïveté, in Mme. de Beau-

Beauty and the Beast: **Jean Marais and Josette Day.**   *G. R. Aldo-Discina*

mont's tale. But in Cocteau's film, this contemplation of the woman one desires, during her entire meal, is a magnificently erotic refinement. And how to describe the scene in which the Beast clasps the quilt that covers Beauty's bed, impregnated with the odor of her skin and her hair, and draws it to his face, breathes into it, buries himself in it? After this scene, we can no longer speak of Mme. de Beaumont. Yes, one last time: at the end of the story, Beauty has decided, on the basis of esteem, gratitude, and friendship, to marry the Beast. She therefore returns to the Beast's château, "attires herself in magnificent robes to please him, and is bored to death all day, waiting for nine in the evening. . . ." The Beast does not appear, and Beauty, frantic, finally finds him, "stretched out, unconscious and she feared he was dead. She threw herself on his body without thought of his beastly form; and, feeling that his heart was still beating, she took water from the canal and dashed it on his face." Jean Cocteau, of course, cut out the final dialogue between the Beast and Beauty; in the film Beauty and Beast speak to each other as little as possible, and it is above all by her expression that Beauty conveys her love to the dying Beast. But he did not actually repeat—and it's astonishing—Beauty's rush to fling herself on the Beast, nor did he repeat the gesture of the water. All the importance is thus concentrated on the Beast's expression in this instant, an expression that Cocteau had extraordinarily foreseen and visualized in the scenario of *The Blood of a Poet*: at the moment of the child's death, the black angel—shot as a negative in the scene—"colossal, sprawling, crushed against the pale pilgrim, turns backward toward the audience the face of a dying animal." And it is the Beast's tearful glances, his manner of listening, his voice, his eagerness for the least caress, his patience, his gestures of love and of vanquished animal that make him so touching, whereas his moments as a murderous and ferocious animal render him more pathetic than horrible. The Beast, beneath all the exterior trappings, is exposed. Cocteau created him as a great lord; Bérard and Marais endowed him with nobility, presence, hauteur, and strength, and then, all at once, we discover the lost, pitiable Beast, withdrawing to lick his wounds, humiliated, his eyes downcast, after Beauty has rejected him.

The Beast then is in essence a Cocteau character, and one of the most

extraordinary characters in cinema; and in saying this, I am not thinking
of his fantastic side, but of his spiritual and mythical value in the special
universe of Jean Cocteau. Removed from the context of this universe—but
why leave it?—or viewed from the exterior, one has only a drastically re-
duced understanding of the film, and is confronted with the endlessly
seductive snares of symbolism and error. Cocteau, however, quite obviously
detested symbols, and nothing was more foreign to him than the simplifica-
tions of Manichaeism. Unfortunately, this fact doesn't prevent certain individuals in various articles from ceaselessly referring to symbols and to
"the forest of symbols." Avenant is taken to be the human part of man
and the Beast to be the monstrous part, the forces of evil, the instincts, the
Dionysian drives—as if instinct and Dionysian impulses were necessarily
nocturnal and evil! Avenant and the Beast are thus construed as composing
a symbolic double image of man. Beauty is redemption, and from the
double death of which she is supposed to be the cause, springs Prince
Ardent, incorporating the beauty of Avenant and the Beast's qualities of
heart . . . Ardent whom alone, according to this thesis, Beauty can love.
This is what symbolmongers would have us believe, but the amateur
symbolists would do well to reflect, for if one accepts these explanations,
then it is no longer possible to understand anything at all. Is not the
Beast presumed to be the bestial part of man's nature? Yet here he
represents the heart, and Avenant the face merely, and all the complexities
seem to be ignored: Avenant's bad character, his own cruelties, violence,
and perfidious acts, and the fact that his handsomeness had hardly affected
Beauty up to this point; the fact that the Beast is all goodness in Beauty's
presence and all cruelty away from her side; that Alice would have said of
this lordly creature, "for a beast he is very beautiful"; that it is for the
Beast and not for Prince Ardent that Beauty's face has radiated love, and
that it is the Beast who has awakened and moved her. The abstractors of
symbolic quintessence forget the essential mystery of Cocteau, and this
mysteriousness has once again come into play in *Beauty and the Beast*.
Undoubtedly, Jean Cocteau was the first to permit those who prefer
exegetic exercises to the fascination of a visual spectacle to bring to his
work a little of whatever they wanted; he willingly regarded himself as a

Beauty and the Beast: **Jean Marais and Josette Day.**   *G. R. Aldo-Discina*

carpenter making a table, and afterward those who wished were free to place things on that table. For myself, I like to contemplate the naked table in its singular beauty—it is pure and beautiful because it is empty, and I prefer to listen to what is bespoken by its simple garb of beauty freshly plucked from the poet. The table speaks without being touched, in countertime and counter rhythms.

The Beast is a personage common to Jean Cocteau's dramaturgy and to his poetry. The Beast is he who must perish through love, and for the sake of love. From this death is reborn the same being, with the same face, scarcely different to all appearances; it is not a phenomenon of meta-morphosis but of phoenixology, this progression of "other selves" through which the poet, and any person devoted to the fulfillment of his being, must live. From this perspective *Beauty and the Beast* takes its place in the Orphic cycle of Jean Cocteau, and partakes of his other indissoluble themes: resemblances, truth, falsehood. Among Avenant, the Beast, and the Prince, who is the truest and the best? Which of these three lies most nearly approximates the truth? It is with the third, with the third form, that Beauty flies away; might we not wonder whether it is necessary for this prince, too handsome, too charming, too virtuous and too perfect a lover, to rebecome a bit *man* and a bit *Beast* to satisfy Beauty? Yet it is true that they are not of this world, that their kingdom is perhaps one of perfect fulfillment, where perfection is obligatory, that Beauty is also perfect and that, after all, it is the end of the fairy tale, Cocteau having for once avoided a tragic finale. But he was haunted by tragedy, and several months after the completion of the film he conceived another ending in which the fairy tale and its marvels are undone: Beauty's heart and passions were opened to the Beast, and the Beast should therefore remain the Beast and die forever, perhaps because he did not have the right to want so totally to be loved by Beauty. Beauty would remain alone with her memories and mourning.

Beauty and the Beast: **Jean Marais, Michel Auclair, and tavern companions.**
G. R. Aldo-Discina

We shall never have these nocturnal images of Beauty; we are left with the last images of Beauty radiant and illumined, Beauty in sunlight, Beauty like sunlight, and love, and poetry. She is in no way the symbol of purity, love, or poetry. She is a young girl, active and good, sensitive and generous; above all, she is exceptionally beautiful, and all that happens to her happens because she is beautiful; Beauty is a woman. Though Beauty serves in her father's house, it is not as a Cinderella, but because she loves her father, with the kindness, courage, and solidity of a country girl. And though Beauty is assuredly frightened at first sight of the Beast, she quickly regains the country girl's firmness and good, solid courage. But Beauty soon comes to like being afraid, and to enjoy the trembling the Beast evokes in her. Beauty belongs to the kingdom of day, and is held captive

Beauty and the Beast: **Jean Marais, Marcel André, Michel Auclair, and Josette Day.**
G. R. Aldo-Discina

in the kingdom of night, soon voluntarily captive in this palace of night, of which the master himself is a prisoner, for she has sensed that this night is not a total blackness of the soul but that, on the contrary, it allows her own soul to surge forth and breathe freely, for she recognizes in this night and in the Beast much of herself.

And the Beast strongly resembles Beauty. The written account of the fairy tale makes use, as was customary, of several illustrations that are more reminiscent of the traditional Snow White affectations than of the style of Gustave Doré. Who could have foreseen that these twenty pages by Mme. de Beaumont would yield characters like Cocteau's Beauty and Beast? The flat pastel silhouettes of the fairy tale adopt the forms and contours, the plastic and moral values of heroes in the most singular and exceptional dramatic mythology of this century, set forth in magnificently sumptuous imagery, an imagery of exemplary rigor and order, and of superior veracity in depicting both the quotidian and the prodigious. Descendant of Méliès, without a doubt.

Certainly, Jean *The Falconer* carries in the center of his blazon the enameled colors, metals, and reputable credentials of the "sorcerer from Montreuil."[1] But the gold and the intricate form, the principal and outstanding features of this blazon, eloquently attest to the several centuries intervening between Méliès and Cocteau. Méliès was a marvelous necessity, primitive and outlandish; all art is obliged to pass through a period of the mountebank's booth, elaborate exaggeration, and fanfare, through all the moments of an amateur production. With Méliès the fairies are present and visible, the stars are of gilded cardboard, the moon of painted paper, and M. le Baron is hardly phantasmagorical: his belly is obviously cotton batting, he has dined too well, metaphysical anxiety is not his strong point; the terrors here are hardly "holy"; they rather resemble the demons in a medieval miracle play; a kind of locomotion through a childlike cosmos, and when one crosses the portal of a mirror, the paper tears like a circus

---

1 Méliès' studio, the first film studio in the world, was located in the town of Montreuil, a suburb of Paris.—ED.

hoop. One cannot emphasize too strongly the grandeur of this moment, which was to cinema what two centuries of French farce and Italian *commedia* were to Molière; farce and *commedia* allowed Sganarelle to become a great comic character, as Méliès, with his outlandish fairy folk, enabled Jean Cocteau to make this "fairy tale without fairies."

The entire esthetic—and the ethic as well—of *Beauty and the Beast* is summarized in this definition: One must flee the fairies, the poetic, the cleverly contrived, speculative fantasy, the mists and fluctuations of conventional irreality, the better to attain fairyland, poetry, and marvels, finally recognizable as such, through rigor, order, natural invention, beauty, simple lines, or tamed baroque, perfect harmony and rhythms. It is in this quest that one is constantly aware of a Cocteau stretched taut with passion and exigence, all through the "Journal of a Film: *Beauty and the Beast*." In this journal, Cocteau makes frequent reference to *The Blood of a Poet*: "I am obliged to work as I did during the epoch of *The Blood of a Poet,* when nothing could slow me down. This is the price of freshness." He refers also to a certain conception of work that is equally a conception of filmmaking: "It is a workday that I love. Very skillful and very precise." This film was literally snapped from the jaws of seven-headed adversity by fighting every inch of the way. Certain of these threats originated with Cocteau himself: his fears, his audacity, his precautions, this technique which he knew how to improvise, developing it into a style as he went along. He was convinced, for example, that the extremely simple angles and relative immobility of the camera during the scenes in Beauty's house and garden—which Christian Bérard found rather pedestrian at the time— would take on their necessary and singular rhythm when combined with dialogue and with the transitional cuts that he shot in the studio. This was particularly true for the scenes in the Beast's park where the need for another kind of angle was felt, because "it is the Beast and it is Raray,[1]

---

[1] By some unimaginable mass error, stemming from an unidentified article, all the film notices read: "Château de Ratay, Ille-et-Vilaine." But in reality, it is the low wall of the park of Raray, near Senlis. It is Beauty's manor house, Rochecorbon, which is in Ille-et-Vilaine.

the most bizarre park in France," said Cocteau. He knew. He carried within him the revelation of his film; he had received its grace; he had the vision of it; he had faith in this film, and his faith is measured by the disquiet and boldness, the fears and certainties it engendered, and by the risk it involved. In its apparent obviousness, the film was to encounter other difficulties in its reception by the public. *Beauty and the Beast* was either accepted solely on the basis of its formal splendor or, conversely, denounced because of a beauty that, it was contended, froze, petrified the work. For some, the bride was quite lovely, and they forgot the suffering of her origins and her blemishes; for others, she was too beautiful, and her beauty arrested all emotion.

It was at the very interior of his work that Cocteau was attacked, accused of being merely picturesque and "decorative"; in reaction, Cocteau was haunted by memories of *The Blood of a Poet,* obsessed with the need to flee, as in that first film, the poetic and the irreal. Thus the insistently repeated demand that Henri Alekan should photograph "hard," the unflagging attention to the utility of every prop—for everything is a prop and nothing is merely decorative; a chair, a doorway, or a sedan chair either serves a purpose and disappears or never appears at all. In the palace of the Beast, where the walls have eyes, eyes that are intended for seeing, there is not the gesture of a candelabra, not the breath of a caryatid that is not precise and justified, a reaction to an arrival or a presence. Never are these stage props proposed as elements of décor, nor are they presented to the eye for the sake of their fantastic aspect alone. One actually sees very little of them; in the château sequences—where one might most expect and fear (or hope for, according to one's taste) an orgy of visual decoration—there is a certain silence of setting similar to the silence of the text. Nor is there any sign of profusion, delirium, or pomp. If one's glance is invited to linger a moment, it is on a movement or a rhythm—the rhythm of Beauty's entrance, for example, for which Cocteau had the marvelous idea of reusing the "reverse zoom" device of *The Blood of a Poet*—the actress is pulled along on a plank, which in combination with the slight changes in speed, the white veils, the shivering air, and, above all, the beautiful and graceful feet of Josette Day (who was a dancer), achieves a miracle. The miracle of a measure found, tempo held, the equilibrium so dear to Cocteau.

All these qualities reappear, in another light and a different reality, at the house and in the orchard of Beauty's father. Every one of these scenes is resplendent with the beauty of a truth that owes nothing to what is commonly called realism. As one might expect, we shall select the sequence of the sheets for detailed study, specifically because it is extraordinarily beautiful, but also because it is either too often admired for its plastic values alone—abstracted from the context of the scene—admired in its appearances, its attributes, and not for its substance, or else is too often denounced in the name of these same appearances, by the uncritical admirers of the film's formal beauty who, one is tempted to say, denounce this particular sequence only because they recognize and fear its rationale and its virtue. Jean Cocteau mounted this scene with his own hands, sinking the pegs into the ground, stretching the wet sheets taut to increase their transparency, fixing the clothespins, constructing a labyrinthine décor, a theatre of white perspectives, of a beauty bordering on the provocative—and which would indeed be just that if the direction were to play up this beauty. However, the beauty is handled with extreme temperance; it is neither exalted nor transfigured, but presented for what it is, which is much better, and we are not allowed to forget that they are only, after all, sheets hung out to dry. Beauty, clothed like a princess, approaches the sheets, and murmurs: "Who has done my laundry?"—the use of the possessive is marvelous!— ". . . the sheets are poorly hung; they're dragging on the ground," she remarks. It is thus Beauty who affirms the realism of the scene and setting, but by a truthful word, a characteristic comment. Linked to this simple truth, and captured by an absolutely immobile camera, the plastic and rhythmic serenity of this sheet sequence, following the palace scenes, assumes its true value. The beauty of these images, like all those in the film, yet these with even more radiance, moves us to tears.

The complete enchantment that, according to the admirers of *Beauty and the Beast,* comes only after belief, or at least is intimately linked with it, is solely a product of the mobile lights of cinema. There are no set pieces, even in the carefully composed shot in which Ludovic stands before the sheet, Avenant in the corner, lifting a flap of the sheet while, high up in the opposite corner, appear the stupefied faces of Félicie and her sister, topped by the typically Bérardian sunbonnets with pointed crowns; the ridge of the sheet climbs at a gentle oblique angle, separating the faces of the men from those of the women. One doesn't think for a moment of a painting or of a composition and pictorial values; in its equilibriums and in its ordered, internal rhythms this scene achieves such beauty only by virtue of its compositional, balanced, and rhythmical rapports with preceding and succeeding scenes. But this, of course, is the essence of cinema, and Cocteau had sensed intuitively, beginning with *The Blood of a Poet,* that cinema, as François Truffaut loves to say, is first and foremost two shots that follow one after the other, and follow each other well. It is true that the images of *Beauty and the Beast* would not have this ultimate excellence if Cocteau and Bérard had not themselves had the revelations of Jan Vermeer of Delft and Pieter de Hooch on the one hand, and of Gustave Doré on the other. But they re-created nothing in the imagery of paintings: as cultivated men they knew how to observe and forget.

Thus one never feels the desire to make a set piece, and although it sometimes seems that a shot is about to arrange itself into one, it is to reveal to us, in the total movement of the whole scene, a mounting joy and beauty; the scene never stops there—far from it—in fact, it gathers impetus rather than being weighed down, drawing greater strength and nobility from such moments, a more resonant pitch, and then moves on. This is the reason for the exclusive use of fixed shots in the sheet sequence, in which one might have expected the mobility of a camera playing adroitly, too adroitly, over this laundry décor. Instead, Cocteau chose the fixed camera shot, for in his cinematographic writing he studiously avoided decorative frills, and movements around and among the sheeted alleys would have been just that, as are so many zoom shots that create no real or necessary movement or arbitrarily break movement that should otherwise have been continuous. Cocteau detested this kind of shot. At other times—and I am thinking here of the scenes in the interior of Beauty's house where one might expect fixed shots—one sees the camera precipitated in three steps from one character to another, with short, lively, efficient,

Beauty and the Beast: **Mila Parély (back to the camera), Michel Auclair, and
Nane Germon.** *G. R. Aldo-Discina*

and absolutely unspectacular movements. The same kind of camera movements characterizes the scenes of the interior of the caravan in *Les Parents
terribles.*

This is the proper moment to salute Christian Bérard. Cocteau adored
watching Bérard work. He would provoke Bérard into activity by first
devising his own approximate solutions to problems. Bérard would actively
protest these makeshift answers, which he then hastened to correct with
precision and mettle. "He was the only one to understand," says Cocteau,
"that vagueness is unsuitable to the fairy world and that mystery exists
only in precise things. He also recognized that nothing is easier in filmmaking than false fantasy. He avoided it with infallible grace." Christian
Bérard and Jean Cocteau truly had in common the very special gift of
measure and sobriety, a sense of their own measure even in boldness; the
first hint of the baroque is always controlled, always falling well short of
the excesses that one at first believes it cannot avoid. Exalting and temper-
ing one another, they never commit an excess; they possess true luxury.

These governing qualities of a style, forged with care, constancy, and struggle, are also obviously present in the interpretation, the direction of the actors being a major element of this style. Josette Day was to be above all grace and simplicity incarnate—that is to say, all the exquisite intelligence that she was capable of bringing to everything, that Jean Cocteau expected of her. She was all grace and simplicity, and all was grace in her presence. And in the presence of the two sisters, all was marvelously aggressive or ridiculous acidity; Cathos and Magdelon, nasty, like geese, but sometimes beautiful as well.

Most important of all, there is the gift of self that an exceptional actor made to the film and to the author. Without wishing to downplay the physical courage demanded of Jean Marais for his interpretation of the Beast—the four or five hours needed for makeup, the transformation of Marais's face by a kind of reverse evolution into the features of the Beast, the burden of hours spent without being able to grasp anything in his hands and without being able to swallow anything more than a vague liquid—we shall not insist on this aspect of the role in order to avoid, in turn, sounding picturesque. Jean Marais surmounted all these sufferings, all the ill effects, and by virtue of his exemplary conscientiousness, even surpassed the limits of necessity. Cocteau said of him, "His enduring soul has always been an example to me." Above and beyond the trials of the role, it was also necessary to bring to bear here an absolutely singular talent capable of expressing a person and a soul beneath this incarnation of a monster, and one not content merely to embody the monster or to represent him. The voice, the glances, the positions and movements, the bodily displacements, and not the few spoken lines that accompanied the role, accomplished this miracle, and this mask—in the human sense of the term—wedded closely to the contours of Marais's own face, attains in all its animality a troubling resemblance to Marais himself, yielding a terrifying beauty—a reflection of the beauty in the actor's face. Without wishing to play on the first word of the expression, it is through the Beast that Jean Marais became *un monstre sacré,* by spiritual strength, because he is first of all a tragedian—a tragedian who can dispense with text and gestures because he learned, under the strength of Jean Cocteau, how to make a simple, flat character from a fairy tale partake of sacred myth.

This gradual passage from fairy tale to myth is surely the profound essence of Jean Cocteau's film, even though the author retains the story's happy ending and its narrative allure. The world of the fairy tale is simple, transparent, devoid of the problematic; rewards, punishments, and a moral are at its end. The world of myth is complex, and Cocteau complicates it further with his own extremely personal mythology. His invention of Avenant is particularly significant in that it permits the invention of the Pavilion of Diana and the entry of an essential element from his intimate mythology; the world of Diana's Pavilion partakes of the *cité* Monthiers in *Les Enfants terribles* and *The Blood of a Poet,* of the room and of its treasure in *Les Enfants terribles.* Once again we find the snow, the statue who guards the treasure, statue of a goddess, an immortal Minerva. It is here in the pavilion that the true riches of the Beast are to be found, inviolate. His magic wealth is but a means; these are an end, and they were also a beginning. And he who comes to steal the treasure is killed by the statue, pierced by an arrow; from the very moment he seized the golden key, of which, however, he dares not make use, he was condemned, like he who uncovers the child's ace of hearts in *The Blood of a Poet.* This world is the world of all childhood protected and inviolate, which cannot be violated, but only ceaselessly enriched, by all the most secret, most mysterious part of our interior worlds, by our profound sensibility, which, if not violated, constitutes particularly for the poet one of the inexhaustible wellsprings of poetry.

"Not to be admired, but to be believed," wrote Jean Cocteau. Is this not what he wished to attain, and did attain, in *Beauty and the Beast,* as he attained it, less consciously—by intuition alone—in *The Blood of a Poet?* The latter had no single image, no single set of images admirable in itself, which does not only yield to us ample cause for admiration but which also forces our assent, captivates us. The task was more difficult in *Beauty and the Beast,* which yields a sumptuous conspicuousness at first. Thus, in Cocteau's prologue to the film, he deflects the spectator's attention from his own esthetic sensibilities by asking him to suspend disbelief and enter into "Once upon a time." But in order to lead us to believe in the profound aliveness of this film, as he believed in it himself, it was necessary to follow the path of this sensibility, in creating as well as in receiving the film. Very soon along the way, the film encounters the marvelous, never to stray from it, and one believes in *Beauty and the Beast.* One believes in it because it is a very beautiful, very admirable film. Its images and rhythms take their place in the company of the slow and fascinating glimpses of the bestial-fanged monster framed by Murnau's sublime *Nosferatu,* beside the white linen, the heroine's apparitions, the entrance of the three enchanted masts into the deserted port (there, too, the supernatural and the irreal were expressed in the purest and most simple reality); beside the so Murnau-like movements of *Tabu*—the luminous harmonies and cadences of the boat, the canoes and the golden bodies; movements of visually symphonic intoxication. *Beauty and the Beast* stands, too, beside the secularly tragic depths of the most beautiful Eisenstein film, his immolated masterpiece *Que viva Mexico!,* beside the night's-end return of the fishing skiffs in *La Terra trema,* a grandiose moment in the cinema of the fantastic—in the different and best sense of the term—made all of voice, of almost Grecian clamors, of antique ships, of sails furled in the wind, and of violent sea. In this cinema of white veils and black veils, the first great film of Jean Cocteau gained its place in a single fell swoop.

The Infernal Caravan   *Les Parents terribles* [1]

Or Cocteau's blunt encounter with the cinematographic problem of the un-adapted play. Theatre and cinema are lawless cities. Cocteau, the outlaw, knew this. But one always wants us to believe that order reigns therein. Whose order? Each of those who risks himself in these cities of perdition must bring with him his own order for his own use, or lose himself. One neither adapts nor adopts; great creators are procreators as well, not adoptive fathers, and they beget children in their own images.

[1] In French, the word *parents* means not just "parents," but also blood kin, relatives.

The late and lamented André Bazin, who was, thank God, much less serious than he seemed, wrote a long study in 1951 for the review *Esprit,* entitled "Theatre and Cinema," arriving at this conclusion: "Theatre and cinema are the same thing." This goes for *Mourning Becomes Electra, Henry V, Macbeth, Les Parents terribles.* It remains to be proved.

Theatre and cinema are the same thing, yes, a question of loftiness and writing. Ten years after the first production of the play *Les Parents terribles* at the Théâtre des Ambassadeurs, Jean Cocteau with great difficulty produced his play again, but this time for the screen. And this production was designed totally to enhance the play's theatricality. With the exception of two or three lines, which might just as easily have been changed for a revival in the theatre, the text of the play is there, transformed into film dialogues. These dialogues, in their changed dramatic continuity, become a cinematographic production, constituting a film script in four hundred scenes, and this script in turn comprises the text. It was as if the play had been just a dress rehearsal, whereas passage into filmic form allowed for a final twist to the bolts, a definitive tightening up—not in its text, which no longer had anything to lose or gain, but in the players' interpretations and in the scenic movement. This is in contrast, say, to *L'Aigle à deux têtes,* where the scenario was rewritten from the play's text, and an adaptation was made that opened the film wide spatially (which was also the case for *Ruy Blas*).

Cocteau had written for the stage with his accustomed economy of means, with tailored, polished, and direct efficiency: not a superfluous word, not an unnecessary character attribute, not an inessential prop on the set. "My entire method rests in this," he wrote to Jean-Jacques Kihm: "Nothing must be 'decorative' or useless on a theatre stage. A door, a chair must serve a purpose. This is the style of apparatus, of a performance of gymnasts. (The same goes for directing. That's why in my plays no one ever smokes and the characters have no last names. One must be constantly on guard against the awful danger of the picturesque.)" This is really the nubbin of the Cocteau method; it had been true for what he wrote and was true for his cinematographic productions. It is for this reason that his cinematographic writing could coincide so perfectly with what he had previously written without the slightest thought of the cinema. There was no question of thinking theatre or thinking cinema; he didn't have to write or rewrite his play for the cinema because most often his works for the theatre were written in a chain of theatre images, if one may hazard the expression, that fade into one another like his cinematic images. His rhythm for the theatre was that of the cinema, with its tight dialogues and dense little phrases. The play version of *Orpheus,* in 1925, was written that way. Which didn't prevent Cocteau from writing in other ways, that is, in other rhythms, but always with the same tailoring for characters who required it; for example, the queen in *L'Aigle à deux têtes* at a given moment needs to give herself a grand flight of romantic theatrics, or to transport Renaud and Armide to the heights of spoken opera for which the author would have been equally capable of finding appropriate cinematic images.

Some literary critics, Roger Lannes among them, hold *Les Parents terribles* to be Cocteau's chef-d'œuvre for the theatre. On the strict level of cinematographic scripting, his production is absolutely exemplary and is indeed a masterwork. It affirms, scene by scene, that the function of the camera and the function of a certain space have been rigorously determined and structured; and the dialogue is precipitated into this space and toward the camera; elsewhere, camera and space define themselves as a function of the text in terms of position, the limits of their field, their movement or immobility. This theatrical space was even further constricted, even though the locales have been multiplied by the number of rooms in an apartment, for the direction is not at all based on the depth of the field, it always focuses on the characters by pinning them in corners; everything is in corners here, everything is corner and nook, even in the middle of a room, amid this real disorder that is more than mere messiness or a picturesque collection of curios. The abrupt movements of the camera, its displacements, accentuate this approach, as does the selection of shots; but within such a space and such limits, even the notion of an individual shot is erased. Close-ups, medium shots, and two-shots seem equally near, and even when we come upon characters actively engaged, we have the impression that the camera has not drawn back. The scene changes become imperceptible; it's no longer a succession of shots but a succession of rapid glances, sharply attentive and unflinching. The spectator is at the interior, within their walls, invisible and present, but not behind a veil; we are *there, inside,* among the characters; [1] one even has the impression that we're stepping on their toes, and has the desire to say "Excuse me"—and for a number of reasons; how embarrassing it is, for one ought never have to participate so deeply in the intimacies of strangers. One is denied the comfort of the theatre seat or of the point of view of the characters or the director, for the view always is the one from our own eyes, the spectator's point of view—but a spectator *in* the scene—for we too are directed, and we see everything without interruption, everything that one cannot help seeing. For this reason one might well have the impression that this film is "an abundance of close-ups," as someone wrote; one is not aware of the choice of shots, and differences, any more than one is aware of the choice of words in a verse by Racine, because he had the genius of finding the simplest words, which, when placed in a particular context, become unerringly the most beautiful, right, unique, and irreplaceable words. This is equally true for each shot in *Les Parents terribles.* Only the truly great attain this sublime and luminous simplicity.

Out of about four hundred "numbers" contained in this film, then, there are approximately thirty close-ups, among them the famous shot framing Mik and Yvonne at the instant when the former talks of Madeleine to his mother for the first time: above left, only the mouth of Marais appears; to the right below him, only the eyes of Yvonne de Bray. Mik leaps on "Sophie's" bed, filled with joy at the avowal he is about to make. He darkens the room, seizes his mother, wrapping his arms around her from the left, places his left cheek against his mother's, in a close shot that is not yet a close-up. Michel says: "I wouldn't like you to look at me. Together we'll face the window of the building across the street, the night. Coach horses during a halt." Near the end of the avowal we come upon the close-up already described; we see them looking straight ahead,

[1] ". . . to walk among them, to watch them face to face instead of contemplating them at a distance, on a stage," said Cocteau in *Entretiens autour du cinématographe.*

Les Parents terribles: **Jean Marais and Yvonne de Bray.** *Sirius*

one seeing Madeleine, life, love with Madeleine; the other seeing Mik, whom Madeleine is taking from her, and life dispossessed of Mik. Michel, in love, sees with his lips; Yvonne, who can only possess Michel with her eyes, sees with these passionately excessive eyes, wide open on the void. This shot, exceptionally long, ends, the camera gently withdraws, and on Michel's line, "Sophie! are you happy?" Yvonne turns abruptly, violently, revealing her ravaged visage to a frightened Michel; the two faces are now seen in profile; Michel steps back and the panoramic camera withdraws with him, leaving Yvonne, whose voice we hear off camera: "This, then, is my recompense." The dialogue continues, adopting its second tone, and three brief close-ups, Yvonne, Michel, Yvonne, follow, opening the second part of the scene, violent and delirious, in which Yvonne unleashes her emotions.

In a flat or mediocre film there is an infinite—and often unjustified—distance between a close-up and a long shot; here there is no measured distance between the shots of Yvonne and those of the end of the film, because they have the same necessities and respond to the same exigencies, and reveal to us by slightly diverse means the same approach to beings. We are thus with the camera, in the doorway of Yvonne's bedroom, and through the open doors we see the group formed by Michel and Madeleine, Georges and Léo. The camera retreats and reveals Yvonne from the back; she then turns toward the camera, lingers a moment to listen, her face convulsed, and slowly leaves the set, to one side of the camera. She has not taken her eyes from this group; she hears their joy, their relief. A cut to the group, then the camera again frames Yvonne as she enters into our original field of vision, before the chest of drawers. She enters the range of the camera as she left, moving backward, her eyes fixed on the door, withdrawing to the door of the bathroom. Off camera one hears voices and laughter. Following shot: the bathroom, where we see Yvonne, immobile and in profile, in the doorway, casting a last glance toward Léo's bedroom, wherein sit the four others; she enters. During her withdrawal, in two stages, the camera did not simply accompany the character as in an ordinary zoom shot, nor is it substituted for the character to reveal the group of others upon which Yvonne's stare is riveted, as if to say: Mark well the motivation behind what is about to happen; nor, by taking an inverse position, does the camera propose to read the decision on Yvonne's face by advancing in front of her as she backs away. André Bazin was the first to point out the important nuance here in the *Esprit* article mentioned earlier.

Our role as spectator before the film version of *Les Parents terribles* is an exceptional one, created by Jean Cocteau; he makes us participate in his production, writes us into it, directs from our viewpoint and writes with our point of view.

Thus Jean Cocteau avoided the abuse or systematic utilization of close-ups, and hardly ever used field/counter-field. The large majority of shots are two-shots or close-shots, often framing two faces; of the four hundred shots in the whole, one can count approximately sixty-five in which there is camera movement. These movements are often merely short, free panoramics; never descriptives. When necessary, the camera is made mobile in order to pick up a character, in order to move two steps toward him, two steps toward the point at which a character will appear on the scene, follows him a brief moment, then often precedes him a step to reveal a prop which will play in this scene. There is never a movement that lacks justification, that lacks successful and simple efficiency. Take, for example, the direction of the caravan scene, which matches precisely the mobility of those who live there: the characters are not agitated and yet they continually change place—Yvonne less, but one goes to Yvonne and one comes from Yvonne; Mik leaps toward Yvonne. . . . It is somewhat different at Madeleine's—and I'm thinking here of the visit—less because it is an ordered house, but because everyone is somehow nailed down during this sequence. There's also the spiraling staircase that joins Madeleine's living room to her bookbinding workshop and which naturally determines the rare vertical shots, up or down, which are easy, necessary, barely noticed. The entire scene between ignoble Georges and Madeleine, stricken and constrained to submit herself to the lie that is going to overwhelm her before Michel, is shot in close-ups, as is always the case when terrible things are said or are in preparation; the faces then are always close to one another. These things are going to be repeated with Michel, Léo, and

Yvonne, in a horrible scene in which no one, nothing, can move and, in effect, there is not the least camera movement during the entire scene—nearly twenty-five shots. The camera moves only near the end, when Yvonne, preceded by the camera and speaking all the while, detaches herself from the sofa and from Léo who was sitting beside her, and comes to join Michel and Madeleine. In a moment, a panoramic view follows the departure of Yvonne and Michel; that's all. Further, there were barely two movements in the entire scene between Georges and Madeleine, who remain alone while Mik, his mother, and aunt are sent to take tea in the studio; there are three movements before, in the arrival scene; and even these are little more than the sketches of movement—seven out of the seventy-five or eighty shots of the entire visit to Madeleine's place. Movement picks up slightly in the studio, when Léo stays with Madeleine: three movements out of fourteen shots; Léo is about to be upset, and movement comes again from the soul. Cocteau was capable of daring such things, and confronted these stylistic necessities, and as in all perfect and elegant appropriateness of style to its object, this one passes unobserved; one is sensitive to it in a completely syncretic and intuitive manner. It is not apparent except through direct and repeated analysis.

The acting, which one might quite wrongly believe to be a series of responses to a dramatic interpretation of the scene, is in reality largely influenced by the filmic direction itself. Without a doubt, if one is astounded by all that is exceptional in such acting, by its liveliness, its warmth and sincerity, and if there is substantial evidence that the actors, according to Cocteau's formula, "think what they are saying," and do not think about what they are saying, it is because the actors have, not so much the experience, but the testing of stage play; that is, they have tested hundreds of times that which is no longer a role, or even a character, but a part of themselves. Even this was not without danger, as Cocteau well knew, this symbiosis established between actor and character where the two may intertwine too intimately. The cinema permitted Cocteau to polish their performances, to efface, to rub out by new directives, and by a necessarily more rigorous setting, and through the final touches made possible by editing, to erase all traces of rigid technique, habit, and excessive projections of self left over from the theatre.

Les Parents terribles is a film of words; it is still a film of acts, but the spoken word becomes the act. And one cannot move or be moved other than by the word. One turns, and turns in a closed circle. They are four; Léo is the motor that ceaselessly clashes with order and disorder. Nevertheless, the wheel turns and the caravan advances. Add a fifth wheel to this carriage? Impossible or catastrophic. And catastrophe is exactly what ensues.

At the beginning of this essay I was able to write: Jean Cocteau, man of poetic order. It is, in effect, order and the violent, hard outburst of truth that triumph at the end of Jean Cocteau's plays and films. For Patrice and Nathalie as for Renaud and Armide, or for the queen and Stanislas in *L'Aigle à deux têtes*, it is the end of disorder and a crossing over the threshold of order into a new light. Jocasta conducting her son Oedipus to Colonus by her own voice, which Cocteau makes her lend to Antigone, and Yvonne dying and waiting for her son blinded and seduced by love, are a return to order, or an advance toward an order that is finally within reach. At the end of tragedies, order is the affair of death. The poet sacrificing himself to his work, the death of the poet as a sacrifice to the glory of the poet and of his work, is order establishing and fulfilling itself at last, order at last attained.

Georges, Yvonne, Michel, and Léo are all prey to order and disorder. Georges and Yvonne are unmanageable children; they are childish souls, creatures of naïveté, purity, even in their lies, capable of giving, of generosity, of enthusiasm, and of the greatest forgiveness, but equally capable of the most terrible harshness, by their terrible innocence and egoism. They are the sort of creatures one wouldn't want to meet in real life unless one has as a creed what Jean Cocteau wrote, on another subject, in "Journal de *la Belle et la Bête*": "One must not complain. Pay. Take all the risks." Léo counts herself—alas! she says—among the grownups. But she is the dwarf Achille,[1] the devil, evil—she is the gods. She manipulates

1 Reference to the malevolent figure in *The Eternal Return.*—ED.

Les Parents terribles: **Marcel André and Gabrielle Dorziat.** *Sirius*

everything; she is fate or its instrument, its delegate; in the final analysis she is more dreadful in her arrogance than either Georges or Yvonne.

The opening of *Les Parents terribles* is Racinian: anguish, waiting; something has happened this past night. Yvonne-Agrippine awaits the appearance of her son that morning so that she might ask what he has done with his night, what forbidden Juno retained him. In the first act, catastrophe declares itself, names itself and opens, on all tones, on all dramatic modes. It is the explosion of truth, the act of truth. The second act is the battle against this truth, act of the false. The false neither explodes nor splatters. The light shed by the first act is very hard on other eyes, insupportable, while it holds a terrible fascination for Michel. In the second act the shades have been lowered, and everything possible has been thrown over this light to trample and diffuse it. (Cocteau hated that, even in the cinematic image.) A plot is woven against truth, against love, against life. But is it not against the love of Yvonne and the life of Yvonne that this truth has declared itself? In the third act the light reappears, but it is another light that comes from a greater distance, from the deepest recesses of Léo and Yvonne. No longer the light of candor which shone in the first act: this new light shines deaf, implacable, mighty and destructive. This time everything is pierced through, and the characters are at last fulfilled by their creator. When Yvonne, pressed, cornered, hemmed in by Léo and Georges, grants her assent, she is finished in the other sense of the term. She has been gently dying since she learned of Michel's love for Madeleine; this acceptance torn from her is the final *coup de grâce;* and they do not know it. As if she could, in her passion, actually agree to share, in unequal portions, Michel with a young woman,

Les Parents terribles: **Yvonne de Bray and Gabrielle Dorziat.**   *Sirius*

how can one believe this Yes, in such profound contradiction with all that moves and governs Yvonne?

Yvonne is a magnificent tragic figure. It must be said frankly and strongly that in French dramaturgy the tragic character did not die with Phèdre in 1677. This character is the equal of the greatest of them, composed of obscure and ingenuous passion, of absurdity and tangled reason, of rectitude and madness, of consuming black sorcery and childish joys, of open generosity and grasping jealousy, of extralucid intuition and deaf blindness. Her death is a completion and not an accident. We cannot play on the word; there is only one sense here; this character is terrible.

Léo is another form of the tragic figure, for she is multiform. Her taste for order, present amid such a disorder that it ought to have been forever lost because she lived in it, is more than formidable. It is a tragic sign, the sign that she is to be the instrument of fatality. Léo's order and the contradictions into which she fearlessly flings herself ("It's my own personal disorder," says she), this order is complex, obscure, and terrifying to her. For order always contradicts itself, is a contradiction in itself; it can be born only through the organization of symbols, the pretend-organization of mystery which, in fact, exceeds us. Léo's order is that of the gods. Think of her pose at the death of Yvonne: a statue.

Georges: weakness and shame. He is simply all men. "Poor, poor, poor men," as Nemesis exclaimed at the end of the second act of *La Machine infernal,* having shed her sphinx form. That too is terrible. Michel then is the hero (which is to say, the victim), Oedipus and Orpheus, by turns suffering and glorious, blinded by light and with pierced eyes, entering the terrible path of reestablished order. Who would have the impudence, the levity, to believe that the happiness of Michel and Madeleine is assured? Who would be too blind to have seen that Michel is a marked man, that all the snares are set and cocked, that Michel has dangerously pretended with hubris to affirm his own life, and that Yvonne awaits him?

This is tragedy. But there is never one of those exterior clues that have almost become vulgar billboard proclamations since the eighteenth century. Here tragedy is not declared, not named. It is present, naked, true. Like the style, also nakedly true, and trembling in its nakedness.

Beyond the Glass Curtain   *The Orphic cycle*

"Die and become."
—GOETHE

Because every man should write a Faust, Cocteau wrote three: *The Blood of a Poet, Orpheus, Testament of Orpheus.* The first is a draft of genius, the second a work of classic perfection, the third returns to the source—the river of harmony and splendor of *Orpheus* draws out from the 1930 film all that it possessed of the primitive, in the sense of *"émerveillé."*

The Life of an Artist   *The Blood of a Poet*

A munificent celebration of the mysteries. *The Blood of a Poet* had as its first title *The Life of a Poet.* It was the mysteries of New York, the mysteries of Paris—for a moment, even the mysteries of China—it was the perils of Pauline, the adventures of Zorro: masks and revolvers, bloody battles, bandits and lawmen, kidnappings, disappearances, mistaken identities, "whodunits," child rearing, executions and suicides, keyholes, nonreflecting mirrors, marvels of all sorts. They go on endlessly, for this film is the image of one of its images: a spiral without end. In short, of the incredible but true variety. So much for appearances, but if one moves through them, one discovers their symmetry, their repetition in the reverse of the visible, the purity of mirrors. "That which reveals itself is a vision of the invisible," Anaxagoras had already said, but the Greeks have already said everything, and *The Blood of a Poet* is the first marriage of cinema with Greece, and with the gods: sacred marriage of the cinema, wedding of light and blood. Others will say: It is the Passion of the Poet, his path to the cross, his path to glory, in twelve stations. I prefer the mysteries, and let us not play too much on coincidental words. The essential reference is to the marvels of silent cinema, of cinema-spectacle, of the ciné-magic evoked a moment ago. The credits for *The Blood of a Poet* read: "Spectacle by Jean Cocteau." *The Blood of a Poet* is a poem for cinema, a film, and not in the least avant-garde. No rapport with *La Coquille et le clergyman, Le Ballet méchanique,* or even with *Entracte;* but a film in the vanguard of Cocteau's cinematographic work, yes, a film that marks out the trail. A film that traces out the Orphic cycle of Cocteau, and which in a kind of doubling-back process is crossed by the rays of *Orpheus* and the *Testament.* And now more than ever we can dispense— but we always should have—with attempts to explicate *The Blood of a Poet.* Jean Cocteau reports that just after he had finished the film he showed it to a young girl employed in his household, not without a good deal of apprehension and fear of discrediting himself in the eyes of this young person as a rather irresponsible and less than serious man—we must not smile in remembering Molière's cook! At the end of the screening the girl said to him, more struck with wonder than surprise, "I have spent an hour in another world." This world into which *The Blood of a Poet* opens the doors for us, received its proportions, perspectives, depths, and its architecture from *Orpheus* and *The Testament,* for Cocteau the architect began by building the doors. Now it is our knowledge of the films of 1950 and 1960 that has become primary; it is through them that one must open and discover Cocteau's Orphic cycle; just as one ought to read the first slight novels of Balzac, in which the themes of *The Human Comedy* are unconsciously posed, after the great later novels—*The Red Inn* after *Père Goriot. The Blood of a Poet* has become the exit door from the cinematographic work of Jean Cocteau, a codicil written before the Testament itself. But let's come back to the young girl. Contrary to firmly established frivolous opinion, Cocteau did not reply to the famous "Astonish me!" flung at him by Diaghilev. His response to devotees of the surprises and parades of the avant-garde (which in no way describes Diaghilev, who was completely the contrary) was *Plain-Song,* the well-titled poem that rounds *The Cape of Good Hope*: it summarizes the profound themes of Cocteau, in a form that is simple, balanced, clothed—not in tawdry finery or in the evening dress of verse—form and spirit exalted in poetic art in *The Professional Secret* the same year, 1923, a secret that Radiguet and Cocteau cultivated in common. It is the first of those successive deaths and rebirths of the poet—the grand theme of his cinematic Orphic cycle—and this one is of capital importance, his first auto-da-fé, in both senses of the term, literal and historic, a personal act of faith and burning at the stake. And when he chose film as his medium, Cocteau still did not choose to surprise. There are marvels, of course, but nothing surprising, no more than *L'Age d'or* is a surprising film, nothing which seeks at any price to surprise, much less dazzle. All Cocteau's films will remain true to this esthetic of *The Professional Secret,* and each will find its plainsong. "Elegance consists in not surprising," and Cocteau was elegance itself.

Cocteau had received from the Vicomte Charles de Noailles one million francs to produce a film in complete freedom. This Maecenas gave another million, as we know, to Luis Buñuel, who was to transform it into *L'Age d'or.* One dreams, of course, of equal millions for creative liberty falling today to Orson Welles; he no longer hopes for it. Cocteau and Buñuel worked without knowing anything of their mutual activity. For the one as for the other, it was the same invention of a language which the young Spaniard had already approached in *Le Chien andalou,* the same fresh writing, shots that follow each other well, frames that are the match of men and of expression, and images that by their content are images of a poem. But Cocteau's images live essentially by interlinking, hyphenated with his anterior work and with the personal mythology already constructed in his earlier work. Cocteau played with one finger, as he himself said, a theme that he would orchestrate in *Orpheus.* One finger, obviously, is saying too little, but in any event, from this sonata on, Cocteau would gradually arrive at the grand arrangements of his major works. One must

The Blood of a Poet:
In the background,
Jean Desbordes.

Sacha Mansour

allow me the liberty to affirm that the itinerary of Buñuel is exactly the
inverse, that he would never again achieve the heights of *L'Age d'or,* one
of the most beautiful and greatest films in the world. Further, the images
of poetry in this film surpass all those of *The Blood of a Poet.* Cocteau
knew this, and moreover the images were foreign to him: the cry of Buñuel
was Lorca plus Dali circa 1930; Cocteau was Cocteau plus Chirico, and
Buñuel's cry was not in his register. Yet he admired images such as this
one, for again it was not evoked with words; one must watch it rise into
view in all its violence and force: a man mad with grief suddenly tills the
floor of his chamber with a plowshare. No, it must be seen, and in context, to know that there are very few images, even from the greatest poets,
of this sudden power, of such unique rightness.

Thus Buñuel and Cocteau achieved simultaneously—the first his masterwork, the second a prelude—a first exploration, an initial speleological

descent into the abyss of the poetic *condition,* the first attempt to respond to questions that I shall voluntarily pose in simple fashion: Where does poetry come from? How does it work? What is a poet? In *The Blood of a Poet,* Cocteau organizes the associations—thus we are quite far from surrealism—associations of acts, and not of ideas, and Cocteau's first film was already a film of acts, rising backward in time from fresh memories and from the active play of present preoccupations. How many more or less Freudian skeleton keys have been twisted out of shape in the locks of the Hôtel des Folies Dramatiques, when the doors were open and the keys in the doors, or at least lying on the door mat. *The Blood of a Poet* is an open work; *Orpheus* will be a closed work, but Cocteau extends his hand to us; we cross the threshold; we enter. *The Blood of a Poet* addressed itself in all candor to friends of the first hour, to those who had already read, heard, and discovered Cocteau. And they recognized everything: the theme of the destiny of the poet first broached in *Le Rappel à l'ordre,* treated in the theatre with *Orpheus;* the already mythic theme of Dargelos and the city of Monthiers, of the snowball fight, the theme of the angel who has already appeared in *Le Discours du grand sommeil,* poems of war, the primary experience of death, of suffering, before the deaths of Apollinaire and Radiguet. All this is spontaneously readable, decipherable; the poem is a crest, and one recognizes all the heraldic insignia. And the others, those who were not friends of the first hour? It is even simpler: The film must be viewed in the admirable and fecund stupor of children who recite the fables of La Fontaine, or in the wonder of the young girl mentioned earlier, letting the film act on oneself by letting oneself act through it. In short, one can oneself be sufficiently rich in interior experiences and dreams to dream the film subjectively, to submit it to and identify it with one's own experiences, to reconstruct it, remake the film for which Cocteau gives us the raw materials, which is only another and different way to rejoin the real purpose of this poem of the cinema—Cocteau expected to see diverse paths open up—a way that the friends of the first hour would not fail to borrow. All these attitudes being nothing more than the assurance of becoming friends of the second hour.

In January, 1932, presenting his film at the Vieux-Colombier, Cocteau said: "With this film, we kill death, we kill literature, we make poetry live with a direct life."

Rise of the Phoenix   *Orpheus*

Rise of the phoenix, or phoenixology too. Sounds like the title of a Charlie Parker number. Cocteau loved jazz . . . and cock-and-bull stories. There were thirty-seven *Amphitryon*s before the thirty-eighth by Giraudoux; how many *Orpheus*es before those by Cocteau?

In 1925 Cocteau published the magnificent poem *L'Ange Heurtebise,* and wrote his play *Orpheus,* which was performed for the first time on June 17, 1926, under the aegis of Georges Pitoëff. Marcel Herrand played the role of the angel Heurtebise, which was to be played by Jean Cocteau in a revival. In 1950, this *Orpheus* became a film.

Jean Cocteau reworked his play for the film, not to adapt it but because he wished to bring certain changes to it, for the play was vintage 1925, and if he had written it for the first time in 1950, it would have been what the scenario of the film is. In the play, Orpheus finds a talking horse that brings him in touch with mystery and with the unknown by saying these words to him: "Mme. Eurydice will return from hell." This phrase disturbs Eurydice and fascinates Orpheus, who decides to send nothing but these few words to the annual poetry competition. He is ready to foreswear the honor of being selected the greatest national poet for the sake of this horse. Heurtebise, a rather strange glazier, becomes Eurydice's confidant. It is the angel Heurtebise, the angel of their destiny. Aglaonice directs the literary club of Bacchantes; she now detests Eurydice as much as she does Orpheus; she poisons Eurydice; dying, Eurydice pleads that someone go to find Orpheus. Death enters—a young woman in an evening dress—and steals Eurydice. Heurtebise will aid the desperate Orpheus to descend to Hell, by entering the mirror. Death's proposition is the same as that of the legend, but it is in the midst of an argument after they have already regained earth—there are always arguments in the plays of Cocteau!—that Orpheus stumbles, and in righting himself he turns, only to see Eurydice disappear forever. Aglaonice incites the Bacchantes against Orpheus, for the five initial letters of the famous phrase [1] sent to the competition have deeply insulted the jury Femina. The Bacchantes, led by Aglaonice, storm the house of Orpheus, demanding his death. Orpheus decides not to flee, but to meet death in order to rejoin Eurydice; he dies. The terrified Bacchantes declare to the police that, clamoring beneath Orpheus's balcony, they saw him fall and kill himself. The police arrive at the house of Orpheus and wish to detain Heurtebise. But Heurtebise is *undetainable,* irreal in his real presence; the drama cannot be seized by the mind; nothing is true; all investigation of reason is here condemned to failure, and Heurtebise disappears, leaving these men of the kingdom of the living to lose themselves irretrievably in the traps of reasoning reason. He rejoins Orpheus and Eurydice in that universe to which he had first conducted Orpheus, where time is abolished.

On the stage as well as on film, Cocteau knew equally well how to hit upon an appropriate language for the direct expression of mystery, without recourse to clever artifices, and it is always the most ingenuous, the most luminous simplicity, and the most difficult as well. In this way, Cocteau linked himself firmly to the perfectly classic ideal: to make, with difficulty, easy things, things that will deliver themselves up, completed, under the most successful forms of a clear simplicity. As Orpheus and Heurtebise prepare to step through the mirror into the beyond, Orpheus says "Perhaps I'll be there a long time." "Long for you," replies Heurtebise. "For us it will be as if you entered, only to turn around and step out again." They pass through the mirror as the mailman drops a letter through the slot. The curtain descends slowly and is quickly raised again: the interval. The play was billed as: a tragedy in one act and an interval. When Orpheus and Heurtebise return with Eurydice, the mailman scene is repeated in exact detail: it is the same, in the same time. There is no time beyond the mirror, for beyond there is eternity, the world of eternity:

[1] "Mme. Eurydice reviendra des enfers."

the absence of time and not infinite time. In the film we find the mailman again, with the addition of the clock striking six, and which strikes six again as the voyagers return from the beyond.

If *Les Parents terribles* was transposed into cinema by the grace of Cocteau, and if it found its fulfillment there, *Orpheus* was a play that invoked the cinema with all its force, a force as yet unrealized, precisely that one might believe in that force, just as *The Blood of a Poet* waited to be revived, reengendered, and integrated by rebirth into a completed film. Thus the one-act play becomes on film the great play in five acts, at the same time shedding the mantle of theatre that heretofore had persistently cloaked a truth that was unable to disclose its nakedness on the stage. The first act is an operatic overture: The themes of the real and the irreal are here introduced in their both obvious and mysterious relationship and

Orpheus: **François Périer and Marie Déa before the tribunal in the Zone.**

Discina

all the elements are articulated—the motorcyclists, the Princess, the chalet, Cégeste who is reborn into another life on the outskirts of death, the mirror, the return of Orpheus led by Heurtebise. In the second act, the dangers announce themselves: Heurtebise is going to love Eurydice, who loves Orpheus, who is going to love the Princess, who is forbidden to love Orpheus but who, each night, comes to contemplate Orpheus as he sleeps. The Bacchantes and the avant-garde poets hate Orpheus and unleash their fury upon him, holding him responsible for the disappearance of Cégeste, while at the same time Orpheus is pursuing the Princess through the deserted Parisian landscape that becomes another world and another reality into which we enter without suffering the artificial estrangement of fabricated fantasy. Cocteau simply makes us aware of another reality that "habit hides beneath a dust sheet and prevents us from seeing." And so following the third act, the death of Eurydice, we will discover the Zone without spectacular surprise, and we will quit it unscathed, living with Orpheus and Eurydice by turns in a climate of comedy and then of tragedy. This time Eurydice desires to die, and finds her death. The Princess and Orpheus love each other with a love yet menaced. The fifth act is par excellence a finale of action: the Bacchantes and the young poets attack the house of Orpheus and kill him. His body is borne to the "chalet" by Heurtebise, while the Princess and Cégeste wait in the Zone for the return of Orpheus and Heurtebise by way of a journey that is difficult for Orpheus. Aided by Heurtebise and Cégeste, the Princess revives Orpheus and immolates herself in the immortality to which she brings him, sacrificing herself by love to the glory of the poet. There is nothing left for her but to depart with Heurtebise toward the awful punishment that they have incurred and that is unthinkable in human or earthly terms.

In fact, then, Cocteau has told a well-structured story, such as the French public loves, a strange story but perfectly comprehensible at first encounter and yielding up a sufficient amount of its substance at first reading, a film perfect in its form and in a classic form, a film of admirable images that often meet with equal beauty the music of Georges Auric—the French public adores having a beautiful image and recalling that the music was beautiful as well. It is a film acted with exemplary perfection, and the French public is most appreciative of a play or film that is well acted. For the title (the name of Orpheus enjoying hazy but real popularity), for the magic of the title, for Marais, for Cocteau (whose name also held magic in its own way and excited a variety of reactions—but reactions nonetheless, which is essential), and because the first spectators discovered a film that presented itself in the fashion described above—for all these reasons, the public went to see *Orpheus.*

The *tout Paris* audience present at the elegant premieres received the film rather coolly. The real public proclaimed *Orpheus* a success; obviously it didn't hold the record for box-office receipts in 1950–1951, but neither was it the failure one might have predicted. Cocteau's preceding films had been, in the eyes of the general public, handsome films with everything necessary to please. Such was the feeling toward *Beauty and the Beast, Ruy Blas, L'Aigle à deux têtes,* and, although somewhat different and with some reticence, *Les Parents terribles:* big-name stars, interesting stories, beautiful pictures. Cocteau himself had the pleasant idea of referring to *Orpheus* as a "detective film, bathed on one side," he added, "in myth, and on the other in the supernatural." And certainly the film does set forth the succession of questions common to a mystery film: Where is Cégeste? Who killed Cégeste? Who are this mysterious princess and her acolyte? Who are these death-dealing motorcyclists? . . . questions that are quickly outdistanced by the film. But it is no less certain that those who went to see *Orpheus,* without knowing of Cocteau except through two or three previous films—or being ignorant of him altogether—were led beyond the scheme of the story line, beyond the simple beauty of the images (but certainly by means of the latter) into direct contact with the essential presence and quality of all mystery. There were many, too, who experienced irritation or dissatisfaction at having thus been abandoned to a mystery to which they were aware they did not hold the keys, and to which keys did exist.

We have said that *Orpheus* is a more closed work than *The Blood of a Poet,* though not in the least hermetic or esoteric—nor was *The Blood of a Poet* arcane in its manner, for it more or less permitted us to open whichever doors we pleased. It is the poem as created object that reflects in all ways, by its manner of being and by the way it is made, the poet its creator, but which each spectator is capable of recognizing and deciphering based on what he projects into it himself. It must be said that, most of the time, he will find there what the poet had projected into it of his own being. Poet and spectator together pass through the same mirror, find themselves together in the same hallway of the Hôtel des Folies Dramatiques, knock their heads together trying to peek through the same keyhole at the same time. It is there, however, that they are liable not to see precisely the same things, but it is of no importance. The poem bursts forth through all the outlets it can find, flowing through the profound or superficial, secret or open life of the poet, and through the mythology engendered by that life, and is finally recognized for what it is by the spectator. Nor is *Orpheus* a secret work, but the path of access is neither easy nor leisurely. Here the poet points out the route, but one must tread it carefully, go back over it, as one goes back to a painting, an opera, a tragedy.

On the first run through, whatever our situation vis à vis Cocteau's complete works, one receives the film first of all on the level of a story, an unadorned story. This is a fortuitous circumstance and the very sign of the work's success: It presents us with persons and not with symbols, allegories, or representations. "In *Orpheus*," said Jean Cocteau, "there are neither symbols nor theses. Symbolist works, or those predicted on theses, are out of style in the gravest sense of the term." To begin with, there is the poet, Orpheus, who could be no one other than Orpheus if Cocteau wanted the poet to be believable. This poet has just as much need to believe in himself as the spectator does to believe in him, and never to cease believing that he is *the poet*. It is ever necessary to surpass oneself, to seek and discover, never to sit down or become comfortable, to compose with the glory and exigencies of youth, "to burn alive in order to be reborn," to raze the very nooks in which one longs to find repose, to free oneself by fire from the "entourage of others" in which we dwell, in order to find oneself at last alone within oneself, and in the heart of poetry. "I say that I am born as many and die but one," wrote Valéry. So was Orpheus captivated by the mysterious messages transmitted to him by the Princess's car radio. This radio and this car assure a liaison between the poet and another world; in point of fact they are snares set by Orpheus's death, returning in the guise of a foreign princess to a world of which she is no longer a part, and yet of which she still experiences the passions. But Orpheus, gripped by the new poetic state induced by these messages, sets off on this new itinerary. He pursues the Princess, listens to her, tracks down the unknown, to use his phrase. He hurls himself, without steering, into the life-and-death curve, for there is yet another bridge to be burned: "My life became inebriated, cooked through," says he to Eurydice; "it began to stink of success and honors." If Orpheus suddenly believes that he no longer loves Eurydice and that he does love the Princess, it is because he recognizes in the latter one of his possible forms and at the same time a means of attaining that form. It is less her that he wishes to possess than through her and with her to possess new truths. Through the Princess, Orpheus perceives what he does not know and ardently desires to know. Through Orpheus, whom she loves, the Princess perceives once more what she used to know and knows no longer, what she no longer has the right to know. Through her, Orpheus looks to the future; through him the Princess contemplates the past. It is as dangerous for the one as for the other, though perhaps a bit more so for the Princess. For Orpheus, the primary attraction of the world of the "Zone" is not that it offers an opportunity to explore the kingdom of the dead or its frontiers, but the fact that it is a world from whence springs poetry, in which reside poetic forces—the poetic "exhalation," a world in which the Potomak lives, this monster transmitter of poetry, this radio transmitter of poetry, an errant zone of the spirit, of the absolute poetic state. For Orpheus it is an adventure, and an adventure of life and enrichment. The myth itself is considerably enriched by Cocteau as well, as is always the case each time an ancient myth is inter-worked with his dramaturgy and his poetry.

The fable of Orpheus is no longer anything more than a support, the launching pad, as it were, for Cocteau's own tremendous enthusiasm. It is a great musical movement scored for all his themes, and among them the theme posed, for the first time as a cinematic poem, in *The Blood of a*

Poet, an interrogation on poetry and the poetic state: poetry put to the test. But here it is the inquisitor who suffers torture: "Poetry is indispensable. To what I don't know. It inhabited me, tortured and burned me . . . , I was the vehicle of a force which desired to live in my stead. Let poetry live then, she'll see what it's like!" Elsewhere Cocteau speaks again of this force: "The poet is the servant of a force that he scarcely understands." What is this force, seductive and awesome, where does it come from, precisely where does it lead, and how? These are the questions which the poet of the 1930 film asks himself, as does the poet of the 1950 film. To these questions, Greek antiquity had responded in a more clearly mythical manner; after Plato (Ion), the Romans took up the myth again (Callimachus), and in turn Ronsard in one of his Pindaric odes: from their father, Zeus, the Muses obtain the power to inspire poets of pure heart with their "divine fury." Orpheus and Homer are the first to be touched, the first of the elect, the first to collect the messages transmitted by the "Apollonian chain."

In Cocteau's version, Orpheus is not content to receive, to be elected and inspired in his youth, as Ronsard paints him, evoking his accession to poetry. A new and violent desire to know more seizes Orpheus, a non-intellectual desire. It is an entrancing curiosity, which buffets and teases; Orpheus would know a new poetic truth, that is to say, to take and possess it, to love it. But this time Cocteau has shaken up the myths; the Zone from which come the messages is the fringe of a beyond to which Orpheus is drawn by the snares of the Princess who is *his* death. He is led there by an aide of the Princess, and because of the death of Eurydice, which the Princess had provoked—as she had caused the death of Cégeste, and it is by Cégeste's messages that she captures Orpheus. As in the most ancient Hindu hymns, the metaphysic of Orpheus-Cocteau is simply a questioning, and thus a ceaseless, endless process: Who is this princess? What are these messages? What is poetry and what is it's source? and Who am I—I, the poet, and who is this god? That is essentially what motivates Orpheus and how he conquers his death, how the death of Orpheus conquers the poet she has begun to love. She appears to Orpheus as the visible god who conducts the elect to the god invisible. But all this is Ramakrishna, and one is also reminded of this Hindu prayer:

> "Make me go from nonbeing to being;
> Make me go from obscurity to the light;
> Make me go from death to immortality."

Nevertheless, the encounter is not complete. For the poet must also find the supreme path to knowledge, where reason no longer moves and thought is in repose. Cocteau remains essentially Occidental, bathed in the Greek Mediterranean, and for him it is less important to understand noumenal truth than simply to know the mystery of poetry, its soul, its night, so that one's essence and the essence of poetry become one and the same, and are recognized together, and all the other poets salute this unity with this pure verse by one of today's poets—one of those who hides and preserves himself, and one whom I know—Pierre Matthias:

> "Orpheus, I know you, welcome my comrade."

Like *The Blood of a Poet, Orpheus* is a film about poetry, about its paths and its pace, its fountainheads and deltas, its mysteries and its no less mysterious obviousness, its truths that are truer than the truth, its lies, its severity, its austerity, its terrible demands, its multiple death sentences, its ineffable joys that must be conquered, earned, its voyages, its comings and goings, its round-trip tickets, its ends-of-the-earth, and its just-around-the-corner. This was the drunken adventure of a Rimbaud and his systematic derangement of all the senses so that poetry might reveal to him what our senses record by functional habit without ever really permitting us to see or to hear:

> "And I saw sometimes what man only thinks he has seen."

Rimbaud incinerated himself very quickly and did not wish to be reborn. Cégeste also will not go to the end of his "succession of other selves," of his successive deaths; Cégeste abides in the Zone, while Orpheus is delivered up to the supreme life, as if the young poet had also been sacrificed to the glory of Orpheus. For it is an important nuance in the *Orpheus* of 1950 that Orpheus finds Cégeste at the source of the messages of new poetry, and not exactly Cégeste himself, but simply another poet, young, another moment of poetry, perhaps a mere fashion. Is this a trap, is it a source of truth, the youth that Orpheus has yet to conquer, must ever conquer, which would be a perpetual becoming, to stumble ceaselessly upon the immolated youth of Dargelos, Radiguet, Garros, Desbordes, as well as the youth of Rimbaud and Apollinaire? And it is still Cégeste that Orpheus-Cocteau, in the *Testament,* goes to seek in the limbo where he had left him at the end of *Orpheus;* Cégeste who abides in an unalterable youth perserved from time; Cégeste who gives the poet the hibiscus flower, the creative work, and through it the source of immortality; Cégeste who seems more and more like the poet's own youth, the youth that was, that became, and the youth that was finally conquered, the temple of Diana and its treasures; Cégeste to whom Cocteau gave the name of one of the most beautiful of Greek temples, and which the poet never leaves again, liberated from his death, which was woman and love, and which sacrificed itself for him. Cégeste, radiant in a sort of angelness that makes all things sublime. Hence the ultimate and magnificent necessity of *Testament of Orpheus.* It goes without saying that in all this—the poet of *The Blood of a Poet* was a sculptor, let us remember—the poet is anyone who discovers and accomplishes his *œuvre;* to write, compose, paint, or to create a film can be an act of poetry.

Orpheus is thus the quasi-unique personage of the film, and the others exist only through him and for him. The Princess—the death of Orpheus— is, first of all, beautiful and elegant, like her 1925 counterpart and like the personage in the ballet, *Le Jeune Homme et la Mort.* Cocteau and Bérard had wanted her that way, just as they had rejected anything resembling a Dantesque vision of the Zone. Death is elegant, according to Bérard, "for she has only herself to think of." Drama for the Princess, who is but one of the forms of Death, will come when she ceases to think only of herself, and begins to think of Orpheus, loves him, comes to contemplate him as he sleeps, fixing on him the second gaze stenciled on her eyelids, whose immobility is yet disturbed by the secret life of her subjacent eyes. The

Rolls-Royce is the means of locomotion attributed to her; she must appear a princess; but the chalet already foreshadows the ruins of the Zone; it is a way station, an outpost that is of the first human kingdom, but which mankind has abandoned. Here the Princess has, so to speak, a pied-à-terre. She obeys commandments emanating from forces superior to death and which we cannot know, or else she trangresses, at great risk and peril, perils that are equally unknowable. Speaking to Orpheus of this invisible god, she says: "There are those who believe that he thinks of us, others that he imagines us, and yet others believe that he sleeps forever and that we are his nightmare, his bad dream." But the Princess is visible, and the film makes us believe in this personage and in her comings and goings—as it convinces us from the outset of the necessity of mirrors that span two worlds and of the existence of the Zone—by the absence of any apparatus of the fantastical, by the choice of a truth that imposes itself and sets itself up as reality. Thus we believe in the Princess, and some credit is due to Maria Casarès—but it is Maria Casarès directed by Cocteau, full of contained fire, attaining the life and violence of marble. She forms with Heurtebise a sort of team, two beings roped into the same game and bound by the same action. Heurtebise will also sacrifice himself to Eurydice. Eurydice herself is transparence incarnate—everything travels through her. Orpheus crosses through her without leaving a trace; their house is Eurydice's house in the image of Eurydice, and she moves through everything without seeing, discovering, learning, or knowing. She knows but one thing, her love for Orpheus; it is a transparent block, but a block nonetheless: Eurydice is all of a piece, composed of a single act, the act of love for Orpheus. It is for him that she wishes to disappear a second time and therefore intentionally glances in the rearview mirror of the car so that Orpheus will see her. The rearview mirror is the sort of participating prop that Cocteau loved so well, being himself a mirror; another mirror, another of Death's snares and portals.

Discussing the 1925 version of the play, the critic Henri Bidou spoke of a "meditation on death." It is an incomplete definition of that work and even less applicable to the film, for to rely on it is to lose oneself in metaphysics on the one hand, and on the other to neglect the intimate link between the myth of the poet's destiny and the myth of death that cannot be grasped here except with reference to that destiny. Dreyer, with *Vampyr* and *Ordet,* made metaphysical films; Cocteau did not. In fact, he specifies with regard to the end of the film: "The scene in which one watches the Princess, Heurtebise, and Cégeste inflict on Orpheus the travail by which the Tibetan neophytes are put to sleep that they might travel in time can be taken as death inflicted on a dead man, in order to bring him back to life." Granted, Cocteau was quite capable of choosing this algebra in which less times less makes more in order that Orpheus might be reborn. Jean-Jacques Kihm [1] carried this investigation to an extreme, going as far as the Tibetan *The Book of the Dead,* and examines the film from the point of view of Oriental metaphysics. To me, this is but another case of confusing meditation upon poetry with meditation upon death. In my estimation, there is no indication that Cocteau adhered to this mystique—and admittedly, Kihm doesn't carry it quite that far either. Personally I would retain a simple choice of mythic and plastic themes: the "renaissance" of Orpheus, or before that, his painful march behind Heurtebise in the Zone, where an evil wind is blowing and, in the *Testament,* the disappearance of Cégeste and the poet in the rocky mass of the mountain, like the "radiant bodies" of *The Book of the Dead.* Another similarity: Cocteau and *The Book* share a common conception of a universe of death defined by the abolition of space and time. But for Cocteau, it would be a question of attributing to this universe, of which his fable had need, the same nondimension of space and time found in dreams, in which he situated all the action of *The Blood of a Poet.*

There where Dreyer would have produced a metaphysical film, Cocteau made a film portrait, a film of memories, an incredible, imaginary, and true autobiography. Once again he visits himself. This fidelity of self recurs, needless to say, on the formal level, in this film which abstains from lyricism and any Dantesque vision: "The closer one comes to mystery, the more important it is to be realistic." Christian Bérard had sketched some forty gouaches from which designs the Zone was to be constructed, under his direction. He died, and Cocteau did not wish to confide the task to

[1] *Les Cahiers du Cinéma,* April, 1960.

anyone else; therefore, when he stumbled upon the ruins of the bombarded barracks at Saint-Cyr he adopted them as his Zone, even keeping the train whistles as realistic sounds which take on an irreal quality in the context of the film. The costume of the motorcyclists-killers is in the same spirit: open-necked black shirts, crash helmets and goggles, gauntlets on bare forearms. All that one sees of their faces is inexpressive, closed, blind and deaf; the ensemble is monolithic, inexorable—the violence of death in action. Today one might identify them in appearance and signification with the soldiery invented by Maurice Béjart for the dance of the march in *La Damnation de Faust.* The rigor of the setting is, again, equivalent to that of the scripting, to which one might apply the same conclusions drawn from our analysis of the scripting of *Les Parents terribles.* The camera movements are limited almost exclusively to scenes of the Zone, where we are obliged to discover locales, a room, a tribunal, and where we have to follow the characters on strange paths. As in *The Blood of a Poet* and *Beauty and the Beast,* the trick shots are used as a means of expression, and not to make an impression. By intentional sobriety and abstinence from wild and facile fantasy, or from staginess, by new inventiveness and ingenuity, these shots are true to the tradition of Méliès. Only once, from technical necessity, does Cocteau make use of a special camera and various trick shots, for the march of Orpheus during which he is barely able to keep up with Heurtebise, who seems to walk immobile. Similarly, Cocteau used a special laboratory machine only once in *Beauty and the Beast,* to effect the final lift of the couple into the other kingdom. At times, there are those who have contested, as a mistake and too facile, the landscape shown in negative, through which the Princess's car moves bearing the body of Cégeste, killed by the motorcyclists. But on the contrary, one can perceive here a charming reference, whether conscious or not, to *Nosferatu,* in which the car carrying the film's young hero toward the mysterious chateau also suddenly enters an enchanted forest seen in negative.

This constant care for rigor is concern for the rigor of beauty, and this

Orpheus: **Maria Casarès, Edouard Dermit, François Périer, and Jean Marais in the Zone.**   *Discina*

sense of beauty blazes forth in *Orpheus,* as in *Beauty and the Beast,* exalted by magnificently accidental muic. Nicolas Hayer [1] then brings his immense skill to the perfection of each frame as conceived by Cocteau, and each image arranges itself in cinematic splendor. In *Orpheus,* Jean Cocteau was able to recapture for one of the last times the role of myth. Through myth, all things, all thoughts, all meditation, all reflection, all questioning take on a deformation which yields the most excellent of all possible forms— the strength and countenances that bridge the centuries. Once again, he wished above all to be believed, and he could be believed only through the cinema. He knew this, marveled at cinema to the very end, and chose it for his *Testament.*

His Name Was Jean   *Testament of Orpheus*

A crystalline symmetry of form and shape. With *Testament of Orpheus,* the circle is completed, and Cocteau finishes as he began: by the draft of a film, a film uncompleted, a film "at liberty." And although the material conditions of its production were normal this time, *Testament* becomes once more the film of a craftsman. There was no patron for *Testament* as there had been for *The Blood of a Poet*—the support of five friends, among them Yul Brynner and François Truffaut, was needed before the production was able to find a preliminary base on which to build. A film that presented itself as a veritable adventure as well as being a film about adventures, *Testament* also required a producer who was himself a bold adventurer, a man of culture and taste who had a taste for risk and marvels, in addition to his great admiration for Cocteau and his work. This man was Jean Thuillier. The equilibrium of the thread that draws the hyphen between *The Blood of a Poet* and *Testament* is also perfected, especially on the esthetic plane: The last film takes up the thread of the first, that of a dream, without being the description of a dream any more than that first film had been. This last cinematic poem is composed with the mechanism of dreams. "This film," wrote Cocteau to Jean-Jacques

[1] Director of photography for *Orpheus.*

Kihm on January 31, 1959, "has for a plot the manner in which life charges itself with the nourishment of dreams. Further, my own life is necessarily reflected and interpreted therein, though it is unintentional. Neither head nor tail, but a soul." *The Blood of a Poet* has already been presented as an heraldic shield, which portrayed, in four episodes, the mysteries of the poet's life. Cocteau's definition, among others, of the last film is also the definition of the first.

For the first film, Cocteau had requested an "interpreter" to incarnate the poet—but it was not an actor—and at a turning point in the film the visage of Cocteau suddenly replaces Rivero's mask: "The author snared in the net of his own creation . . ." For The *Testament,* he had also thought first of using an "interpreter," then decided to be the poet himself and to make his debut as an actor at the age of seventy, as he said. An actor who does not act but *is,* this is difficult; Cocteau would perhaps have preferred to act. But neither the poet of 1930 nor the poet of 1960 could have been acted, no more than Cégeste could have been, and therefore none of the three was an actor. In contrast, in a film like *Orpheus,* which is full of dramatic interplay, it was necessary that the poet be played by an actor, who could not conceivably have been anyone other than Jean Marais, the actor whom Cocteau knew and loved above all others, who would be the most attentive, the most responsive, and the most sensitive to his direction.

In the course of the final stroll in *Testament,* Cocteau meets the characters from his previous works, plays, films, drawings, and friends, he crosses his own thoughts, hence his poetry, again and again, and meaures time and space the better to deny and confound them. He escapes from the ordering forces of one world: "in which he well knows he has nothing to do," and in which he can live only as a fraud, encounters his double, who is a forgery despite exterior resemblances, and will not recognize him; he follows Cégeste, who is in fact his true double despite exterior dissimilarities, consents to answer his judges to help them, one would say, in an impossible task, and allows himself to be condemned to life, which at his age, says the judge, Heurtebise, is the minimum penalty. Condemned by his judges, who still have human form and human thoughts, condemned by the gods, who have the form and impassivity of marble and who have no thoughts, but who have a spear, the poet is mistrusted by both men and gods—by the former because they do not understand him, and by the latter because they understand him too well. All the signs and symbols and visages of Cocteau are there, and he himself is wholly present. Some think he is too present, too evident, too ostentatiously set forth in his famous "dangerous visibility," and that his error was to appear in body as well as in spirit— even if it is a fascinating error—that it is therefore the film in which he is least poet and most *chef d'orchestre,* conducting himself at the same time that he conducts the orchestra, marching only to his own beat, accompanied by a whole cortege of characters all too conveniently reassembled through apparently chance encounters.

Certainly, it did require much daring to make this film and to place himself in it body and soul. "As for me, I have everything to lose, and that's why I take the risk," said Cocteau in speaking of *Testament.* More than ever he is here both matter and spirit of his own film; he is not in the least a representation; he does not represent himself but rather presents himself, engaging in the most direct sense of this verb: to make oneself present. Thirty years before, dazzled and impassioned, he had written his first cinematic poem, as he said, with "beings, faces, hands, lights, and objects which one distributes at will." The word-images of his last cinematic poem are also acts, beings, objects immanent in all his being, his life, and his work. Cocteau's hands—in them was his soul, his power, his savoir-faire; his voice, always above or on the side, in the margins; his willowy elegance—the elusive elegance that Cocteau breathed forth, while so many others vainly seek it in oxygen tanks. It was necessary to find the proper locales: an empty movie studio, a few country roads in Provence, the prodigious "halls" of the Baux quarries; the faces, faces of friends, who come to pay a visit to the work and to its master—but which of these two obeys the other?—faces of literary personages, masks, mythical forms, a flower-poem that destroys and then reconstructs itself, lovely and trampled; men-horses—once, no doubt, children who, having played too long at being horses . . . ; atrociously handsome Oedipus, admirable object of horror, the sphinx docilely following the poet who

Testament of Orpheus.

alone has always dominated her; Tiresias, whose three mouths are the mammillae of glory; Pallas-Minerva, reason incarnate, whom one must avoid if the work of flesh and poetry is to be done—offer her nothing and expect nothing from the warrior Pallas but a stab in the back from her spear; the Princess and Heurtebise who between *Orpheus* and *Testament* have been judged and condemned to judge and condemn others; and finally Cégeste.

But before envisaging the presence of Cégeste who has become, as we ought to have suspected by the end of *Orpheus,* a central personage in *Testament,* we greet the gypsies who lament one of the relative deaths of the poet (for Cocteau died when his friends died); if Django had lived, Jean Cocteau would not have neglected to include him among them; Django, of whom he said,[1] "He lived as one dreams of living, in a

[1] In the text of an epigraph to the film of Paul Paviot: *Django Reinhardt.* Reinhardt was a French jazz guitarist of the early part of the century.

caravan . . . he tossed his gold from the windows, and this gold was nought else but himself." This gold which poets mint and which has no market price . . . Even in speaking of his friends Cocteau drew his self-portrait, for the poet loves only those who resemble him—remember the wound-mouth in the hand of *The Blood of a Poet*—and it is Cégeste who resembles the poet, rather than being the poet's double, this double from the Musée Grévin [1] that has always been thrown up to him and that, although disguised in his own features, is yet the falsest possible image of the poet.

Cégeste is the youth of the poet's work, his angel to guard. This true double does not coexist with the poet, but subsists in him; and the poet must strain to identify with him and finally to resemble him. Cégeste was born and reborn from fire and sea, the sea—and not the Ocean—the sea par excellence which runs from Ephesus to Massilia and no farther. Cégeste carries the poet off at the end of the film, snatches him from an order which is not his own and therefore to which he neither owes explanations, nor shows identification papers; he could not be attuned to that order. Cégeste is also present at the opening of the film, even before the credits trace their pure lines of chalk on slate in Cocteau's script, as usual, before the spectacle begins. He watches the Princess and Heurtebise from a great distance; they have been condemned and will never return to the Zone. At what distance in time are they from Cégeste, and from the poet? Cégeste leads the poet to them; there is neither route nor measurable distance nor threshold.

But for this instant—it is a matter of absolute instantaneousness—the poet is gripped by what Cocteau calls "the entanglements of space-time." The very term "entanglement" indicates the tone the author wished to give to these considerations of time and distance. In the chapter "Of Distances," in the *Journal d'un inconnu,* the tone was grave, one might have said that of a sort of poem new for Cocteau, the poem of science. Here he says himself that it is a sort of farce à la Goldoni, opening a film

---

[1] A Paris wax works museum like Mme. Tussaud's in London.—ED.

whose itinerary will adopt a progressive gravity that Cocteau's face will reflect. We have constructed, limited, measured, chronometered a conception of time and space founded on our primary perceptions. In the midst of this century that opened with the blows struck by Einstein on the organization of space heretofore believed immutable and eternal and on the metaphysical truth of time, a century in which the old enigma of time and origins suddenly departs from the metaphysical to repose in the heart of science, in this epoch of non-Aristotelian logic and non-Euclidian geometry, Cocteau pretends to amuse himself by situating his own person in a climate of nontime that of itself destroys the notion of distance. Lost in time that we can know only in a certain continuity called "chronological," the poet, mobile in this space-time, but of a mobility rather poorly controlled, after several false propulsions that throw him either beyond or outside the moment he seeks, is finally able to find the scientist in the precisely utilizable moment of his life, to be sent back by him to our era, returned from intemporality to our reality, shot by a bullet more rapid than light, which kills him in relativity and revives him in his own time, that is to say, in his own and old conception of time. But Cégeste is there to help him escape it once again, this time guiding his steps. Cégeste has knowledge of this other universe.

The Testament is opened, then, we might say, by a fable more than by a farce, but a Socratic fable: "Thou wilt believe it is a fable, but I tell thee that it is a true story," Socrates often says in *Gorgias*, beginning a fabulous story in which he engages his very substance, as does Cocteau in the fabulous story of *Testament*, under the transparent surface of which appears, for the third time, the refracted life and work of the poet. "Every chef d'œuvre is composed of hidden avowals, calculations, proud puns, and strange riddles"; therefore one must mistrust chefs d'œuvre; one quickly embalms them, and mistrusts the poet as one mistrusts the truth. This poet who in 1930 arrives in tatters, scorched alive, to the cinema must inevitably be judged, and his judges don't fail to do so. Cégeste, who insists on bringing him before his judges, does not spare the poet his criticism, but does not judge him. At the scene of the tribunal, Cocteau is before adults. They see only his faults and defects or what appear to them as such. Adults do not appreciate things that seem easy to them (the incredible: I could do as much!), nor those things that seem difficult. That with which his judges reproach him—as does the public that becomes more and more judge and less and less audience, as do the critics who become more and more judges and less and less connoisseurs—what one reproaches him for and what he cultivates is himself.

The poet had been saying the same thing since the *Potomak*. Such is the poet's lot: not facility, but doubt, the fear of being an impostor, the painful necessity of forever being reborn, the refusal to follow the bent of his talents and at the same time to discover limitations that only great artists know how to perceive, and to be wounded by them. How can the poet defend himself? Cocteau predicted this in writing: "The poet will always defend himself poorly at his trial. If he responds well according to the Church, he would betray God." . . . "he is always responsible, but not for that of which he is accused." In any event, he must be condemned, and we meet again the *Hymne de l'automne,* by Ronsard. The trial will be short; like Joan of Arc, the poet will decide to ignore it. He has before him the same judges condemned to judge, the same ill faith, plus bad conscience, for this tribunal is not of the Church. And then, too, the Princess and Heurtebise know him well; at their last meeting the poet was called *Orpheus*. In his very beautiful *Journal d'un inconnu*, the poet had said: "One is either judge or accused. The judge is seated. The accused stands. Live standing." In *Testament,* Cocteau is always standing; he walks ceaselessly, walks, runs; thus he measures, as the Greeks measured the sea; the film is a stroll, as we said earlier; it is entirely in continued movement, a series of acts, acts of the poet, the apostle, and not the acts of a dramatic structure. The poet walks, and as he often repeated—Cocteau loved to repeat himself, and had the strength to do it—he walks with one foot in life, the other in death, like all true poets, as Charlie Chaplin at the end of *The Pilgrim* walked at the frontier, one foot on the United States side and one on the Mexican; on one hand the sheriff, on the other the Mexican bandits; Cocteau between conventional order and the disorder of the avant-garde.

Testament of Orpheus.

Several critics tried to oppose to the images of *Testament* the beauty
of the last scenes of *Orpheus* with which Cocteau opened his last film,
a beauty that in their eyes overshadowed the new scenes that follow and
are not vested with this prestige. To take this point of view is both to be
mistaken about the sense of the beauty of purified splendor of the images
in *Orpheus,* which is neither ornamental nor prestigious, but necessary
to the work, and at the same time to ignore the beauty in the severity of
the images of *Testament.* The exclamation-invocation of Rimbaud, "O my
Good! O my Beautiful!" Cocteau had made his own, and each of his
works had its Good and its Beautiful. The visual splendor of *Orpheus*
is not that of *Beauty and the Beast;* it is just as necessary; it is that of a
grand symphony: *Testament* is an orchestral suite. Did not Cocteau treat
space in juxtapositions creating a new space-fresco made of selected locales
and woven without regard for distances that we are not concerned with
measuring in his film? One may also recall the succession of mansions
in the setting of the mysteries of the Passion and the dreamlike con-
tiguities of the locales. Did he not make use of a new time, time clipped

into pieces and resewn into a patchwork-quilted time? This suite, although orchestrated, whereas the suite of *Beauty and the Beast* was barely so, calls forth its own beauty. Cocteau's search for beauty has something Baudelairian about it: to find a world in which all the correspondences are made, and to find it for each work. Might one not also think, before writing heedlessly on the basis of a superficial impression of contrast, that *Testament* does not reveal to us the same physical countenances as *Orpheus*, that it proposes to us an ambling fable rather than the ordering of a great drama, and that just these reasons lead to another face of the image? Cocteau's theatrical works offer equally these differences of tone and style, but the writing, the quality of writing, remains the same. What is important, and what one must recognize from *Orpheus* to *Testament* is that the writing does not change: always keen, naked, quick, etched. Cocteau was horrified by flowing, curved writing—*de la ronde, de la bâtarde!*—and by professionals, *maîtres d'hôtels,* and schoolmasters of the camera. Here it is the reign of the Doric order, number and stone. Each shot has its golden height where the lines love and take each other, appeased, and the rapports of image and sound are in perfect understanding; as a Cocteau film must be grasped with all the senses to be truly understood.

The Firebrand

It is time to set down some conclusions. The position held by Cocteau, as author of films, is exceptional, unique: he is the only one among the great writers,[1] poets, novelists, and playwrights of this century to have rec-

[1] Malraux, who had a feeling and a taste for cinema, and who was capable of making a single remarkable film, might have been able to be the second. His film, *Espoir,* has rarely been seen in the United States. Although the film—a remarkable, lyrical documentary of the Spanish Civil War—deals with the same events as Malraux's novel of the same name (*Espoir,* translated as *Man's Hope*), the film is not an adaptation of the novel. Rather, these are two major works that examine the war in Spain from different perspectives.

ognized, loved, and adopted the cinema as he did, to have been worthy of it, and to have won a place among the first ranks of the great creators of the cinema. This achievement in itself justifies the importance that we have accorded, and that cannot be ignored, to the rich and unceasing interactions weaving between literature and cinema. He was capable, from his very first contact with filmmaking, of capturing a style that reveals man, remaining true to the general esthetic that he had constructed as early as 1930 and that he strove to protect from the comfortable fluctuations of habit, ever concentrating on the enrichment of nuances required by each work. "What is style? For many people," he replied, "it is a complicated way of saying very simple things. For me, it is a simple way of saying complicated things." It is in this that Cocteau is the most Cartesian of French poets and filmmakers. In France one is never quite certain who is Cartesian; one imagines that the average Frenchman is Cartesian —though one cannot be both Cartesian and average—because when confronted with works of art the Frenchman says: We must understand, explain. What does this mean? What was the artist trying to say? And because he has the taste for a certain petty logic. Cocteau liked to say: "I do not think, therefore I am." His paradoxes were often the best, though curious, paths to a common thought—a thought common to the liveliest, most profound minds of the ages. He was Cartesian in form, then, if not in thought, but that's what counts. With Cocteau everything was light, order, division, progression, in a form of expression proceeding from the thought, or, if one prefers, from the Idea, which in turn is composed of a complex and ever-changing sum of projects under consideration, intuitions, encounters, of everything that would permit Cocteau to say: I do not think. But this form itself expresses something totally interior that was the obscurity, disorder, tumult, multiplication—in short the interior disorder that undoubtedly gripped Descartes and that made method an absolute necessity. Cocteau, too, fully recognized this necessity, saying, "The absence of rules in poetry obliges the poet to find methods for himself. . . ." But in France, one is always confusing rules and methods, hence the misunderstanding.

Cocteau often said, in various ways, that he was governed by mechanics;

these mechanics are never those of habit or profession. To stylistic and thematic constants in his work there corresponds a constant and bold questioning of both style and theme in the new context of each film. No one of his films repeats any other.

Cocteau had no trade, unless it was to live; he made only those films he wanted to make, when he felt that he must make them, and only those films to which he was totally committed; a privileged filmmaker, cinematographer of tomorrow . . . or of never.

A unity of method, of writing, established itself among all the means of expression of which he made use, but for each medium he circumscribed its independence and specific characteristics; this is particularly true of his films, these severely simple texts, films that were conceived exclusively in the pure terms of cinema, even when it was a question of filming one of his own plays.

The cinema of Jean Cocteau is, at the level of creation, a cinema of passion and joy; for him each film was a quest for joy, and was made with joy; it was a festival of the spirit and the heart. Immersed in a film, Cocteau was happy, exalted, feverish to the point of exhaustion. He was happy at the moment of conception of the film, at the scripting, happy during the directing of the film, at the first rushes, at stripping in the sound. This is the joy of a Jean Renoir, who was jubilant, who snorted like Boudu in the Marne. Cocteau didn't snort, but his was essentially the same joy, the same love of actors. Sometimes his joy was a kind of suffering, for he was less of a hedonist than Renoir, and more anxious. Cocteau, man of grave joy and of suffering, and, through these, a man of wisdom. "Through suffering, knowledge"; so said Aeschylus; we must come to Greece, then, at the close of these conclusions. "Hail, O thou who hast suffered pain, that which thou hast never suffered before." That is an Orphic inscription.

It was to André Fraigneau in his *Entretiens à la radio* that Cocteau made his famous reply to the question: If fire broke out in your home, what things would you carry away with you? "I think that I would carry away the fire." There are always strange conjunctions between Cocteau and the Greeks. Hear Heraclitus: "All things are an exchange for fire." And the following, which infuses the Orphic cycle of Cocteau:

"Man is ignited and snuffed out like the light during the night, and it is the same thing in us, that which is living and that which is dead. When men die, things wait for them that they do not foresee and of which they do not dream. . . . Mortals are immortal and the immortals are mortal, each living the death and dying the life of the other. . . . This world that is the same for all, neither god nor man has made it, but it always has been and forever will be a fire eternally living, rhythmically igniting and snuffing itself out."

Jean Cocteau the Greek, the Apollonian. His entire esthetic and moral system is of a Greek order. The measure of which Heraclitus speaks is not that of moderate slopes, it is rhythm, the rhythm of Cocteau. Moderation and equilibrium in form, excess in destinies, as with the Greeks, for Cocteau, too, is of that race of visionaries, and in each of his films there are sudden shrillnesses that are solar, violet; the disequilibrium of destinies that seek their own order, their own temple—immoderation dominated by the playwright. For his life and his art, Cocteau knew how to make his own one of the devices of the seven sages: "Control thyself, shun insolence," for there is also esthetic insolence. "Nothing in excess," that was his other motto, and he sought to divest himself of the excesses of poetry of the image, of its too sensual plasticity, seeking marble, knowing it to be carnal by nature. He belonged to the race of visionaries further by reason of his devotion to myths. This fidelity must not be confused with facility: to reinterpret, to bring alive again, to re-create the greatest myths and abysses of the human spirit to the measure of his own century—this fidelity was that of strength and richness.

To the difficulty of being that he felt so acutely, Cocteau joined the concern and need for the continuity of being. One considers putting this last observation in quotes, for it is reminiscent of Georges Bataille, but for Cocteau this continuity of self finds fulfillment more in the passion of poetry than in Eros, and Cocteau does not have Bataille's taste for death, destruction, and horror. The dialectic of love that is expressed in

Cocteau's films, as in all his work, is platonic; passion, both the object and the subject of all his films—the poet's passion and the poet's view of passion—bursts forth or transcends itself in the mystic and ascetic, becomes a quest for the Absolute, a desire to contemplate the Idea, an eternal union or union in another time, in another place, and if this time and place should be the opposite of life, the inverse of the visible, would not what is revealed be what Anaxagoras called simply a vision of the invisible? This is the question asked in the three Orphic films. Therefore one must not say, as been suggested elsewhere, that Cocteau's work constitutes a condemnation of love. Beginning with *The Blood of a Poet,* there is an uninterrupted upward movement toward an ever more elevated concept of love, the love that requires the transcendence and gift of self, the immolation of self in order to attain to a new self, a new universe, to achieve the height from which one inhales the air of veritable love and not of man's pitiful pretenses in which he—within limits from which he knows not how to escape—is content to exalt himself so theatrically and so ridiculously. Cocteau constantly sought the soul of poetry and of passion, both of which bruised and matured him, as he sought the soul of all things and in all things, and his own soul through all things. "I am now certain that the soul speaks in shadow and in silence," he would say; it is the shadow and the silence of that "night of the human body one calls the soul," night of which the poet is not master. This soul, then, is also the inspiration-expiration, that part of the poet's self that is in communication with the obscure, the nocturnal, the source of all light, of all poetry; it is the hyphen, the link, the wick to which one must dare to set the flame, for the poet must be a firebrand. I love this old expression from mining language: The firebrand; light the fire, carry it away, exchange for the fire—thus we return to Heraclitus, without having left Cocteau.

Testament of Orpheus: Jean Cocteau. The death of the poet. "For a long time I have been preparing myself for the exercise which consists, for the poet, in simulating death."

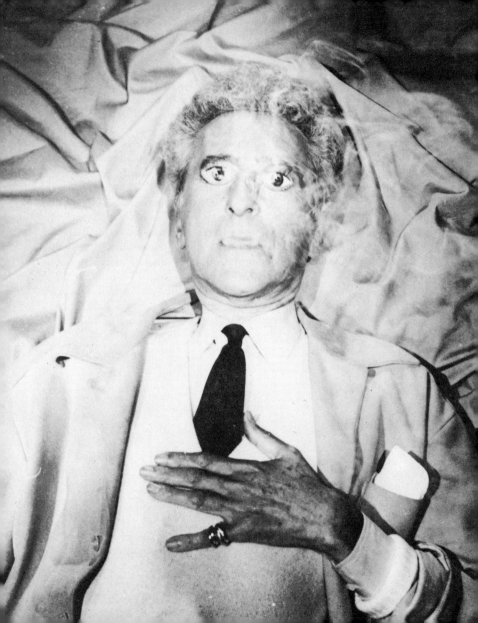

On the tablet of the white screens, Jean Cocteau traced the luminous signs of his poetry, drew his figures and his stars. He dedicated his last work to "the successive generations of youth who have always supported it." He had the happiness to know the presence and attention of the young cinephiles at the *Testament of Orpheus*. This young generation, and those who know how to remain young, like those who illustrate the recent regeneration of French filmmaking, are loyal admirers of the cinematic works of Jean Cocteau. They appreciate his truth and his severity: "My lies are truth. Severity even in dreams . . ." he wrote in one of his grave and transcendent puns from *Opéra,* and we may apply what he said of the music of Erik Satie directly to his own films: "Never any sorcery or patches or false caresses, no fevers, no miasma . . ." It is Dorian harmony, restraining by the blue purity of its equilibrium all the tumultuous instability behind it, and thus creating an order, a morality, a style —in sum a way of life, according to Picasso, who says: "To paint, to write —[let us add, to make films]—that is a way of life." Picasso, of whom his friend Cocteau liked to repeat this aphorism: "It takes a long time to become young." Cocteau became young quickly; he will remain young always; he is young.

TEXTS
Chosen by René Gilson

I am not a writer to order. I write when I cannot not write. The least possible. To write dialogues bores me. But to move this great machine of dreams, to do battle with the angel of light, with the angel of machines, with the angels of space and time, this is work to my measure!

—JEAN COCTEAU

THE CINEMA ACCORDING TO JEAN COCTEAU

CINEMATOGRAPHY VERSUS CINEMA

I purposely use the term "cinematography" in order to avoid confusing the means, the vehicle it represents, with what one commonly refers to as the *cinema,* a dubious muse in the sense that she is incapable of waiting, while all the other muses do wait and should by rights be painted or sculpted in a waiting pose.

What one commonly calls cinema has not been presented, until now, as a pretext for thought. One enters the theatre, glances at the screen (a little), listens (a little), leaves, and forgets. Whereas I believe that cinematography is a powerful weapon for projecting thought, even into a crowd that refuses it.

My primary concern in a film is to prevent the images from flowing together, to oppose them, to anchor and join them without damaging their relief. For it's this deplorable running together that critics of cinematography call "cinema" and that they take to be its style. Today they are wont to say that a film is perhaps good but that "it's not cinema," or that a film lacks beauty but "it's cinema," and so forth. This forces cinematography to be nothing more than distraction rather than a vehicle for thought.

(*Entretiens autour du cinématographe,* Editions André Bonne)

Orson Welles's *Macbeth* leaves the audience deaf and blind, and I believe those who love it (of whom I am proud to be one) are few. Welles shot this film in a great hurry, after innumerable rehearsals. Which is to say he wanted to conserve its theatrical style, seeking to prove that the cinematographer can turn his attention to any and all works and disdain the rhythm that one imagines to be that of cinema. Cinema is an abbreviation I deplore because of what it represents. In Venice we heard this absurd leitmotiv repeated all the time: "That's cinema," or, "That's not cinema." They even added, "This is a good film, but it's not cinema," or, "This film isn't very good, but it's cinema." They heard that we were mocking such comments and, when we were interviewed together on the radio, Welles and I replied that we would be pleased to know what constituted a "cinema film" and that we asked nothing more than to learn the recipe so we could put it into practice.

(Preface to André Bazin's *Orson Welles,* Editions Chavane)

GRAMMAR

The Rules

Don't look at the camera. (False, without the least importance.) The direction of the eyes. (False, without the least importance.) When a character leaves in one direction, he must return from another. (False, without the least importance.) Angles of 180 degrees. The 180-degree angle is taboo. When I decided to use it, everyone's face fell. My assistant and the apprentice assistant said they wouldn't take the responsibility. When the Rolls-Royce carrying Orpheus' body stops on the road, a 380-degree pan raised my young assistants' hair. To be fair, they recognized after the editing that I had been right and that the success of the images we had assembled was due only to this heresy. First image: the Rolls stops, surrounded by its motorcycle guard. Second image (180 degrees): from the opposite direction, one of the motorcyclists approaches the door of the car and questions Heurtebise. Third shot (180 degrees): the camera shows Orpheus in the other direction, stretched out on the car cushions. Fourth image (180 degrees): close-up, again opposite in direction to the preceding shot, shows the head of the dead Orpheus hanging from the seat. The Rolls pulls away, and the camera, shaken by the cut from the close-up of this head to a long shot, shows the car and the motorcyclists who disappear down the highway. Such scandals are the grammar of every pure-bred director. The establishment is bent on banishing them. The young directors, excited by Orson Welles, Ford, or the Italians, still don't dare to cross them. When are we going to give them a hand camera and order them to forget all rules except the ones they invent for themselves as they write and not to fear spelling mistakes? Not that I recommend spelling mistakes, but anything is better than an academism that plays false behind the spurious novelty of cinematographic education.

(Entretiens autour du cinématographe, ed. cit.)

Is a man capable of piercing the mystery I analyze, and of mastering it? No. Technique itself is a trap. Wilde aptly remarked that technique is only individuality. The technicians for my film *Beauty and the Beast* claimed that I had a first-class technique. I have none. Because there is none. Doubtless one calls technique the instantaneous equilibriums the mind instinctively sets in motion in order to avoid breaking its neck. This is what Picasso sums up in his great phrase: "A *métier* is that which cannot be learned."

(La Difficulté d'être, Editions du Rocher)

The Image

I slept little. The film was shown, and advertised its faults. Alekan is afraid. He hesitates. He doesn't dare work in hardness. The result is a certain flabbiness that I must correct in his work. It's all too pretty. I would like it to be rougher, with more contrasts. I'll badger him until he comes round.

After the screening, I scold Alekan, whose mania for weaving and diffusing revolts me. It's the artistical genre. Nothing is worth the sublimation of the documentary style. It's this style that I want to obtain from him.

Alekan said that at the studio people are saying that everything I find admirable is inept, poorly lit, cream cheese. Why doesn't he know yet what I've been accustomed to for years? Every time one tries something different, people become blind, they see only that which resembles what they've already seen. People have firmly decided that anything that's fuzzy is poetic. However, in my eyes, poetry is precision, numbers, and I push Alekan toward the inverse of what seems poetic to these imbeciles. He's a bit troubled. He doesn't yet have my long habit of battle, my serenity in face of the foolishness of the time.

Nothing seems more dismal to me than the photographic unity of a film, a unity the specialists mistake for style. A film should distract the eye by contrasts, by effects that look, not to copy those of nature, but rather to find that truth which Goethe opposed to nature. . . .

It will happen that I light one face more than another, light a room more than it ought to be or less, give a candle the power of a lamp. For the park of the Beast, I adopt a sort of twilight that hardly corresponds to the hour at which Beauty takes her walk. I may even link this twilight with some moonlight if I need it. But it's not because I'm dealing with a fairyland that I make use of fantasy so liberally, along with realism.

A film is writing in images, and I seek to communicate a mood that corresponds to feelings more than to facts.

(Journal de la Belle et la Bête, Editions du Rocher)

Acting

I have great difficulty in making the actors understand that the film's style requires a supernatural relief and absence of the natural. One speaks little. One does not permit oneself the slightest blurring. The sentences are very short and very precise. The abruptness of these phrases, which disconcerts the actors and prevents them from "acting," form in ensemble the cogwheels of a great machine, whose details are incomprehensible. There are moments when I am ashamed to insist on a discipline they accept only because of their confidence in me. Their confidence robs me of my own and makes me fear that I am unworthy of it.

(Ibid)

Editing

Except in rare circumstances, traveling shots annul movement. If you follow a racehorse, it runs standing still. If the same horse passes twenty times before a fixed camera placed at different angles, its speed becomes apparent and multiplied tenfold. In *Les Parents terribles* the camera moves very little. But I frequently change the angles. In the queen's chamber in *L'Aigle à deux têtes,* where Edwige Feuillère endlessly paces up and down the room, moving away from and deeper back into the silences of Jean Marais, I used this system, which didn't take its definitive form until the editing. Editing is style. A filmmaker who doesn't do his own editing is translated into a foreign language; but I've already said that.

(Entretiens autour du cinématographe, ed. cit.)

Cinematography is the craft of editing. Editing is the most important work of the filmmaker. It's his style and his signature. The manner of splicing the images one to another sets the film's rhythm. I believe that one might imagine an internal mechanism similar to this external one. One might also seek an internal method of expression for the cinematographer comparable to editing. And here I seem to be indicting myself, since in a manner of speaking I cinematographized a play in the case of *Les Parents terribles* . . . no longer through a keyhole but by walking about beneath the actors' noses, looking close into their faces. The angles of cinematography thus allowed me to view cinematographically a play as the theatregoer never sees it, because he is too far away in his seat. But I imagine that one might go much more deeply in this research and that one might discover a mechanism of the soul that is not a mechanism of words, a nocturnal mechanism, to shed light on the details of night, in the same way that one edits a film.

(*Cinéma, un œil ouvert sur le monde,* Editions Clairefontaine)

THE PUBLIC AND THE JUDGES

Once upon a time the artist found himself faced with silence; today, that silence makes a terrible noise. Everyone is mixed up in everything. It's the fault of the Encyclopedists, who complained that the pastry cooks judged them. Diderot makes note of it. This complaint is curious, since it is the Encyclopedists who killed the élite and declared that everyone has the right to think. The result is, in 1951, that even stupidity thinks. Which never happened before. In Paris, the élite audience believes that they could do better than the author and act better than the players. There is no longer a public. There are only judges. An individualistic crowd, a crowd unsuited to collective hypnosis, without which a spectacle has no *raison d'être.* This stiffening against a work of art ceases as soon as the mass public comes to see it. They've paid and want to see a spectacle. Thus it's not the masses I incriminate, but this false élite that has insinuated itself between us and the masses. Living, as they do, by fashion, as soon as a production does not fit what is believed to be the current mode, the false élite decides it is outmoded. Naturally! It is as outmoded as is anything of value that refuses to obey the verdicts of foolishness.

The difference is that in 1930 this public was scandalized; in 1951 it is disdainful. It has taken the bull by the horns. It is the jury of the tribunal. What would happen to us if we didn't have our court of appeals in the mass public, and abroad, where our little disputes ring only faintly? . . .

A. F.[1] Given the tremendous success it [*Beauty and the Beast*] had with the large public, had you foreseen in adapting this fable that there was an unconscious demand for it?

J. C. I did not feel very sure of this, since the film's first public exposure, at the Cannes Festival, barely escaped disaster. The august body of judges ruled that the film would go over the heads of children and would seem childish to adults. The extraordinary success of the film began after this obstacle that is always thrown up to us and that so disturbed my production director that he begged me to cut one of the best scenes in the film, only to ask me to reinsert it three years later.

A. F. This experience might have led you to believe that the public expected such things from you. Why have you changed since then?

J. C. It is not up to us to obey the public, which doesn't know what it wants, but to oblige the public to follow us. If it refuses, we must use ruses: images, stars, settings, and other magic lanterns suitable to intrigue children and to make them swallow the spectacle. As long as they don't instantly eliminate it, the beneficial poison enters into the organism. Little by little the cancer of foolishness is attenuated and, in certain rare cases, cured. I've seen it happen.

                    (*Entretiens autour du cinématographe, ed. cit.*)

REALITY AND TRUTH

. . . . The idea of realism forms in the minds of our judges only when they are faced with the life of the streets and slums. Thus they

---

[1] André Fraigneau, interviewer in *Entretiens autour du cinématographe*.

have baptized as "neorealist" the films in which our Italian comrades deploy a kind of imagination analogous to that of Arab storytellers. . . . For me, and without a shadow of paradox, *Beauty and the Beast, L'Aigle à deux têtes,* and *Orpheus* are realist films in the same measure as *Les Parents terribles,* for the excellent reason that all films are realist because they *show* things instead of suggesting them by a written text. Whatever one sees one sees. And it therefore becomes true, in the sense in which Goethe employs the term.

. . . . Goethe opposes this "truth" by which the artist expresses himself, and even expresses his lies, to the "reality" that would offer only a flat copy of its models. One recalls the anecdote in which Goethe presents Eckerman with an engraving of Rubens, and asks him if he understands why Goethe finds it beautiful. Eckerman (naturally) says no, which (naturally) allows Goethe to point out to him that the shadow of sheep that ought to have been on the left is on the right and that by this subterfuge the artist has dominated nature and expressed himself. I was wrong then to speak of realism; "verism" is the right word. Not that one attempts to approximate a verity that does not objectively exist, but that one attempts to approximate a subjective verity, a verity that is one's own.

. . . . The strength of a film rests in its verism. I mean that one doesn't tell things, one shows them. They exist therefore as facts, even if these facts make the irreal into real substance which the public is not accustomed to. I remember a film club that showed Leni Riefenstahl's film *Olympia*[1] last year. The drama of this film is that it is the dead who act and that a dreadful foot had stirred up the anthills. The young audience was particularly restless, responding as they were to the political associations and implications of the film.

However, within a few minutes, the film began to hold them solely

[1] A brilliant, if somewhat ponderous, documentary of the 1936 Olympics. The film is widely believed to be Nazi propaganda for Aryan youth, but in fairness it must be said that some of the film's most impressive moments follow the grace of the great Jesse Owens and other black American athletes.—ED.

on the strength of its verism. It became *a newsreel*. The audience became impassioned by the athletes, by the competition, and forgot that this competition was old, destroyed, dissolved. What one believed, one saw. This verism of moving images overcame everything else. The crowd of spectators became a stadium crowd and not a film club. This is extremely important. It proves that film authorizes us to express anything at all, provided that we can imbue it with an expressive force sufficient to transmute our phantasms into undeniable facts.

If our figures weaken and our problem is stated without being resolved, the public is not present before a distinct, superior fact. It becomes aware of technique, aware of the mise en scène, and refuses to believe in it. Technique and direction must evaporate in favor of a truth that is our own and that must convince the eye, the ear, and the soul. . . .

(Ibid.)

I should like people to find my images realistic. If I annoy everyone with my trick shots—you've seen what it's like—it's because I want the true irreal that allows all of us to dream the same dream together. This is not the dream of sleep. It's the waking dream, irreal realism, more true than the truth. One day people will see that this realism is the distinctive sign of our generation.

(To François-Régis Bastide)

THE PATHS OF POETRY

I believe that the great cinematographic privilege of France is poetry. France is a country that detests poets, but it is a nation of poets. This is a great contradiction, but it can be understood. In effect, a poet can work only in a state of conflict and, to a certain extent, only when he is "doubled." [1] In France one is always being "doubled." Yet, poetry always comes out of it. When I admire a painter, I'm told, "Yes, that's

1 A term used in the game of bridge. A player may "double" an opponent's bid if he believes he can defeat it. If the doubled bid remains unchanged and is defeated in the play, there are extra penalties. Thus, to "double" is to challenge.—ED.

handsome, but it's not painting." When I admire an athlete like Al Brown, I'm told, "Yes that's handsome, but it's not sport." And when I admire a film, I'm told, "Yes that's handsome, but it's not cinema." So I began to wonder what it was. I was told, "It's something else." I finished by discovering that this "something else" is a very good definition of poetry. This other thing is the thing that counts. For one must not mistake the poetic for poetry. There is in France an internal, mysterious poetry that sometimes expresses itself, alas, poetically. The poetic has nothing whatsoever to do with poetry. But I believe that there are extraordinary wellsprings of poetry in France. I became conscious of it when I made a film like *Beauty and the Beast* or like *Orpheus,* and even when I made a film like *The Eternal Return,* with Jean Delannoy.

. . . . The public believes that, if the language is not poetic, it is not a film of poetry. Whereas a poet ought not to concern himself with poetry; poetry should burst forth of its own accord. The text should be very dry and simple. Poetry should spring from the organization of images. The curious thing is that one always confuses the cabinetmaker with the spiritualist. Quite obviously, it's not the same thing. I make a table, and what happens to this table afterward is not my concern. I am a worker in wood. Then the spiritualists come; they place their hands on the table and try to make it speak. Either the table speaks or it doesn't. But it is very rare to find a carpenter-spiritualist. It's as if you asked the flowers to read treatises on horticulture. The poet must be able to set in motion an unconsciousness that doesn't let him think too much. He must express himself in a sort of hypnosis, a kind of sleep.

Take care! I don't believe in this fashionable term "evasion." I believe in invasion. I believe that instead of evading oneself through a work one is invaded by it. I mean the same thing when I say, "There is no inspiration; there is only expiration." That is, inspiration would come from outside, and there is no outside. It is your night that speaks, things in yourself that you do not know. Thus there is an expiration. We've been mistaken on the terms. Evasion is a joke. What is beautiful is to be invaded, inhabited, disturbed, obsessed, deranged by a work.

The public doesn't like the rules to be changed. But what is a poet? He's a man who changes the rules. He's a man who puts his foot in it. My method has always been to put my feet in it. Not on purpose. But if I am holed up in the country and I write a play or a film, I become aware afterward that I've put my feet in it. I would be a coward if I did this work in a closet. I must display it. Putting my feet into it attracts problems for me, but that is unimportant. We are dead men vis-à-vis a work we have written, since after the words "the end," the I who wrote the work is dead. The work is posthumous. The blows rained down on us afterward are like knocking on a tomb. This is what gives me, by the way, a certain respect for the things I have written or filmed, since I have no respect for art. I consider art an expression of the individual, like the shoots from a seed, and I don't imagine a plant respects itself.

(*Cinéma, un œil ouvert sur le monde, ed. cit.*)

. . . . A film, to be commercially exploited, must be at least 7,848 feet long. It's not a good length: too long to correspond to a short story and too short to correspond to a novel. It doesn't matter. That's the length. One must stick to it. While I was filming *Beauty and the Beast,* the principle anxiety of our studio management was that I would make it too short. It did me no good to reply by my particular methods; the figures contradicted me, and they were law. The film became shorter. The faces became longer. I continued to go my way.

A film is composed of longs and shorts. It has an internal rhythm. Numbers don't recognize that rhythm. The accountants' accountings were correct. So were mine.[1] On the last day, when I questioned my script girl

---

[1] Do two and two make four? Gustave de Rothschild said: "Two and two make twenty-two." And two chairs plus two apples do not make four.

as to the balance between the paper (which is one thing) and the action (which is another), she replied, astounded, that I had made it. I was left with two scenes in reserve. But, without knowing the figures, I had decided the evening before to shoot two additional scenes. The length of the film, which I refused to drag out, remained to be seen. End to end, cut, spliced and respliced it had exactly the prescribed 7,848 feet. Not one more, not one less.

I report this incident, in which I appear to play the hero's part, only to give an example, taken from life, of a victory over arithmetic by the numbers that live within us and calculate themselves. Poetry is nothing more than numbers, algebra, geometry, arithmetic, and proofs. Only, neither its numbers nor its proofs are seen.

(La Difficulté d'être)

My method is simple: not to mix myself into poetry. It must come of itself. Even to hear its name whispered frightens it away. I try to make a table. It's up to you thereafter to eat off it, question it, or make firewood out of it.

(Journal de la Belle et la Bête)

Too much solicitude, any door opened at random, frightens poetry, already so difficult to snare. One tames it with a bit of the unexpected. Trees where trees shouldn't be, an object that changes its place, a lifted hat that finds itself back on a head; in short, a crack in the wall and poetry penetrates. Those who pick up on these spelling mistakes are those who read poorly, and are not fascinated by the story. No importance.

(Ibid.)

WHAT IT MEANS TO FILM

"Keep the Secret"

A long time ago I saw in a catalog of come-ons for weddings and banquets: "a hard thing to find." I don't know what this object is and what it's called, but I'm glad it exists, and I dream about it. A work of art ought to be "a hard thing to find." It ought to defend itself against vulgar contacts, the rough handling that tarnishes and deforms it. It should be impossible to know how to approach it, a phenomenon that annoys the critics, aggravates them, incites them to insult, but preserves the work's freshness. The less it is compromised, the less quickly it opens its petals, the less quickly it fades. A work must make contact, even if it be through misunderstanding, and hide its riches, which will reveal themselves little by little, very slowly. A work that guards no secret and that gives itself too quickly runs the strong risk of being snuffed out and of leaving nothing of itself but a withered stalk.

(Entretiens autour du cinématographe, ed. cit.)

Descent into Oneself

. . . . It is probable that the phrase "Therefore write of the marvelous in cinematography" derives from the films *The Blood of a Poet* and *Beauty and the Beast,* which were conceived fifteen years apart, and in both of which one agrees to see the workings of this curiosity that pushes us to open forbidden doors, to sing as we walk into the night to keep up our courage.

Now, *The Blood of a Poet* is nothing other than a descent into oneself, a way to employ the mechanism of dreams without sleeping, an awkward candle often snuffed out by a breath, carried through the night of the human body. Acts link themselves there as they wish, under such faint controls that one couldn't possibly attribute the process to the mind. Rather attribute it to a kind of sleepwalking state that encourages the profusion of free memories to combine, knot, and deform themselves until they take a shape strange to us and become an enigma.

Nowhere less appropriate than France for the exercise of that faculty which has recourse to neither symbol nor reason. Few Frenchmen want to enjoy an exceptional event without knowing its source and purpose, nor do they want to study it. They prefer to laugh and examine it with insults.

The symbol is their last resort. It gives them scope. It allows them to explain the incomprehensible and to clothe with a hidden meaning the thing that draws its beauty from having none. "Why? Are you joking? Whom are you trying to fool?" are the weapons France opposes to the wholly new form that a proud soul assumes when it manifests itself, against all expectations, and intrigues a few interested individuals.

(La Difficulté d'être, op. cit.)

Those Things That Had a Meaning

When I said on television and radio that my film *Testament of Orpheus* "would have neither head nor tail, but a soul," I was joking without really joking. In truth I am astonished: In an era where painters have sacrificed subject matter to the art of painting and have abolished the model or the pretext for painting, filmmakers—harassed by producers who "know" that the public is a many-headed child who wants someone to tell him a story— insist on a "subject" and a *pretext,* whereas the manner of telling, and of showing things and of furnishing the screen, is a thousand times more important than what is told there.

Alas! the public (and that of films is vast) is still like the lady who, disliking the Zouaves, declares herself unable to like Van Gogh's Zouave, or like the man allergic to roses, who couldn't possibly hang on his wall a bouquet of roses by Fantin-Latour or Renoir.

But the hour has come to destroy these ridiculous taboos and to educate film audiences in the same way that audiences have been educated to exhibitions of painting. Otherwise the youth of the cinematographic milieu will never be young, and will be condemned forever to obey the bad habits of producers, distributors, and theatre managers.

It is ridiculous to say that cinema has nothing to do with the rare and strange. Such a statement denies cinema the role of Muse. For the Muses should be portrayed in the position of waiting. They wait for beauty, disconcerting at first contact, and seemingly ugly, slowly to penetrate our spirits. Alas! the absurd sums that cinema costs oblige it to bow before the idol of the immediate.

It is this hideous idol of our era, this detestable dogma that must be vanquished. It can't be done in a single blow. But I shall be proud if my effort counts for something and if one future day youth owes me a little for being able to bring out a film as a poet publishes a book of poems, without being condemned to the American imperative of best seller.

. . . . My anticartesianism is so strong that I have become its Descartes.

To the degree that I respect the partly open circle of Pascal, into which chance may penetrate by surprise, so much do I detest the closed circle of a scientist—at variance, in fact, with the actual progress of science—which symbolizes the horrible mania of the French to want to understand everything. Why? That's the leitmotiv of France: "Explain to me what you were trying to say, what you were trying to paint." A little more and it would be necessary to explain what music means. As in the *Symphonie Pastorale,* when the audience delights in identifying the cuckoo and the peasant rondos.

Anything that explains itself or justifies itself is vulgar. Men will have to admit that they inhabit an incomprehensible planet on which they walk upside down in relation to the natives of the antipodes, and that infinity, eternity, space-time, and other phantasms will remain forever incomprehensible to our infirm intelligence, confined to three dimensions, even if the poor terrestrials tear themselves painfully from the earth (to which they will remain attached by an umbilical cord) and visit the moon, which is an ancient, dead earth and not much farther from us than Asnières or Bois-Colombes.[1]

. . . . It is certain that the large majority of those who see my film [*Testament of Orpheus*] will say that it is foolishness and that one can

[1] Suburbs of Paris.—TRANS.

understand nothing of it. They won't be completely wrong, for there are times when I understand nothing of it myself and am on the verge of abandoning ship and apologizing to those who believed in me. But experience having taught me that one must not under any circumstances renounce those things that once had a sense and that seem to lose it, I seek to conquer my weakness and to assert the confidence in myself that I feel vis-à-vis others, if I admire and respect them. In short, I trust in that *other*, in that stranger that we become a few moments after having created a work of art.

The first question the journalists ask me is that famous French question "What's the story?" And if I reply with frankness, "There is none," they regard me with the fear one feels in the face of madness. And the reply is exact. *There is none.* I avail myself of the realism of places, persons, gestures, words, and music in order to mold a form for abstract thought—and, I might add, to construct a château, without which one can ill imagine a phantom. If the château is itself misty and evanescent, the phantom within looses its power to materialize and to frighten.

(*Le Monde,* July 25, 1959)

The Marriage of the Concrete and the Unconscious

Do *you* understand? [1] Raoul Lévy told me that no one would understand my film at all! But do *you* understand something of it? I read this little fairy tale ten years ago in children's books. Whom is it going to astonish! He told me that no one would understand, that they look for symbols. . . .

But of course, my film is full of symbols, if you like, but since I'm not conscious of it, they're no longer symbols. Symbols of what? People will see what they see. They'll see a peculiar-looking dog, for example; they'll want to laugh and won't dare to; they'll scratch their heads, wondering what it symbolizes; at that moment I pass by, glance at the dog and say, "What a strange dog!" Because I smiled, they don't laugh, right? I detest picturesqueness, the fantastical, symbols, all those old sheet anchors the public clings to for fear it will tumble from its quotidian comfort into the ocean

[1] Various of Cocteau's comments during the filming of *Testament of Orpheus,* directed to and reported by François-Régis Bastide.

of things that disturb it and that it avoids for fear of drowning. There is nothing more glorious than being shipwrecked, than disobeying dead rules, than accident and errors, if man is strong enough to sanctify them and turn them into archetypes. An error ceases to be an error if the one who errs transforms it into what Baudelaire called "the most recent expression of Beauty."

. . . . I worked thirty years to make this film, in which I organize acts as one organizes words to construct a poem. In some ways it is a transmutation of word into deed. Here, words are without importance. Only action counts; I tell no story.

I let events follow the path of their own choosing. But instead of losing all control, as happens in a dream, I celebrate the marriage of the concrete and the unconscious, which gives birth to the terrible and delightful beast *Poetry*.

Only, one always makes this mistake: to confuse this beast with its mimic, with its shadow play, with the poetic, which is as far removed from poetry as were *"les precieuses ridicules"* [1] from Mme. de La Fayette.

(*Les Lettres françaises,* Oct. 8, 1959)

It stands to reason that film, by virtue of the possibilities it offers to restage time and to conquer its narrow limitations, was the only language suitable for bringing my night into the light of day, for placing it on a table in full view. Moreover, this feeling was not mine alone.

. . . . I'm conscious of the fact that I demand a tremendous effort from the public and that it would be ridiculous to pretend that the audience will take the trouble to untangle a skein I don't untangle myself. Only, it sometimes happens that one allows oneself to become bewitched by an enigmatic atmosphere (that of dreams, among others); and I believe that a

---

[1] The title of the first prose comedy by Molière (1659), in which he ridiculed the manners of his time, particularly the excessively refined jargon of provincial women who attempted to imitate the manners of the *haut monde.*—TRANS.

work of art can intrigue without being compromised, can be binding without being proved arithmetically or submitted to verification of the golden number.

(Arts, February 10, 1960)

EXCERPTS FROM SCREEN PLAYS

THE BLOOD OF A POET

The Passage Through the Mirror

AUTHOR'S VOICE: *The next morning . . .*

The camera shows, from top to bottom, from a distance and in the light of dawn, the table on which the poet has fallen asleep, his head resting in profile on his arm, with the hand open. Sound effects: swallows. The scream of a train. Cockcrow.

TEXT (the author's handwriting): *The surprises of photography, or how I let myself be caught up in my own film.*

(The author's signature.)

The camera shows a close shot of the sleeping poet, become a plaster figure of the author, resting on a plaster arm, a plaster hand open and extended. In the palm of this hand, the mouth dreams. It breathes gently. It whispers meaningless words.

The poet awakens. Taken from the other side, the shot shows the poet's back and, in the middle distance, between the window and the washstand, the plaster statue of a woman, without arms, draped in plaster, life size. The poet rises. He holds his right elbow with his left hand.

He advances, slightly bent over, toward the statue, as if she were asleep and he were afraid of waking her.

The statue. The poet circles her and, with the swift movement of an assassin gagging his victim, slaps his right hand across her mouth.

AUTHOR'S VOICE: *It is already dangerous enough to wipe oneself against the furniture. Is he not mad to waken statues with a start from their worldly sleep?*

Close-up of the arm. The effort causes the veins to appear, sketched along the arm like the branches of a tree.

Close-up of the hand and the face of the statue. The statue opens her eyes, that is, the eyes are drawn on the globe of the eyelids. The hand withdraws. The statue moves. Her mouth is alive.

The camera shows the poet examining his clean hand, rid of its wound. He wipes it. He snaps his fingers at the statue. He withdraws from her.

AUTHOR'S VOICE: *Second episode: Do the walls have ears?*

The statue speaks: *Do you really believe it is so simple to rid oneself of a wound, to close the mouth of a wound?*

While the statue speaks, the camera reveals the rest of the room in a sweep. Nothing remains but the walls without windows or door. The poet skirts the walls, tapping them, arrives next to a full-length standing mirror occupying the place where the door used to be. He turns around and . . .

In close-up, cries to the statue (with the author's voice): *Open up!*

Close-up of the face of the ironic statue. She speaks: *One resort is left to you. Enter the mirror and walk about in it.*

Close-up of the poet. He speaks: *You can't enter a mirror.*

Close-up of the statue: *My congratulations. You wrote that one entered mirrors and you didn't believe it.*

Close-up of the poet. Gesture of anger: *I . . .*

Close-up of the statue. She cuts him short: *Try. You can always try . . .*

The poet stands before the mirror. A chair forms beside the frame of the mirror. The poet starts.

Jean Cocteau during the filming of *The Blood of a Poet.* Sacha Mansour

The poet fearfully tests his chair. He circles it. He stands on it. He touches the mirror. His ring hits against it three times, but the knocks are heard later than the contact.

The poet hesitates, looks to the left, places one foot on the frame of the mirror, then the other. He seizes the frame of the mirror with both hands.

Shot of the poet from the waist up and of his reflection in the mirror.

He is looking at the reflection itself, rather than looking at himself in the mirror. VOICE OF THE STATUE: *Try* . . .

Long shot of the mirror. The poet plunges into the glass. The cry of a crowd at a fireworks display accompanies his disappearance.

(They substituted a vat of water for the mirror, fixed the props above it, and nailed the chair on the left. The special effects camera is placed perpendicular to the ensemble. The actor dives. The image righted and quickly cut completes the trompe-l'œil.)

Interior of the mirror. Night. In the distance the poet advances, immobile, on an invisible sliding plank that drifts with him gently to the right and to the left. He approaches, arms raised, his face illuminated from below, until he blocks out the lens.

We switch to the hallway of an obscure hotel. Sordid wallpaper. Linoleum passageway. Doors. Shoes set out in front of the doors. Wall at the end of the hall, which turns to the left.

VOICE OF THE AUTHOR (between the shots of the poet blocking the lens and the shot of the hallway): *The interior of the mirror led to the Hôtel des Folies-Dramatiques.*

An Asiatic in European clothing comes around the corner at the end of the hallway. He is reading a newspaper. He stops in front of a door (the third) and speaks through it, in Chinese. Then he resumes his walk and his newspaper. The paper has been conjured away by the time he disappears from view. Enter the poet, his back to the camera. His gait should be odd because of disequilibrium and a heavy slowness. He is about to pass the first door on the left. He listens. He stops. He kneels. He presses his eye to the keyhole.

Close-up of the poet (face and hands) as he presses his eye to the keyhole.

ORPHEUS

The Death of Eurydice

Orpheus has met the princess, who is his own death. He is obsessed with her, and his wife, Eurydice, suffers, despite the appeasements of Heurtebise, the princess's chauffeur who is assigned to watch over Orpheus.

Fade

The fade opens on the nocturnal bedchamber. The Death of Orpheus, at the foot of the bed, in close-up, with eyes painted on her eyelids.

VOICE OF THE AUTHOR: *And every night the Death of Orpheus returned to the bedchamber.*

Fade

The living room of Orpheus' house

HEURTEBISE: *No, Eurydice, no . . .*

EURYDICE: *I will go, Heurtebise. I will go to Aglaonice's house. I must. Only she will know how to advise me.*

HEURTEBISE: *Orpheus would hate such a step.*

EURYDICE: *Orpheus doesn't care about anything except that woman's car.*

HEURTEBISE: *And even if I agreed to drive you into town, Orpheus is in the garage. He would see you leave.*

EURYDICE: *I'll go by bicycle. I'm used to it.*

HEURTEBISE: *That's ridiculous, in your condition.*

VOICE OF EURYDICE: *I will go.*

HEURTEBISE: *Eurydice! It's not for me to forbid you, but if I beg you?*

Eurydice moves away toward the door to the front steps.

EURYDICE: *I'll go anyway. You won't stop me. I'm going mad.* She exits.

HEURTEBISE (on the steps): *Aglaonice will tell you nothing you don't know, and you'll be dead tired . . .*

He comes back into the room. Distant backfire of motorcycles. He approaches the window. From outside we see his horrified expression. Terrible skidding noise.

Flash to the edge of the road (embankment) in front of Orpheus' house. The bicycle, rolling by itself, turns over and the motorcyclists disappear in the distance. Flash to Orpheus in the car, inside the garage, hunched over the radio. Shortwave.

Lap Dissolve

Orpheus' bedchamber, Heurtebise enters through the trapdoor, carrying Eurydice's body. He approaches the bed, and lays her on it. The light changes. The Princess emerges from the triple mirror, pushing open the right and left partitions. It is she who illumines whatever she approaches.

PRINCESS: *Come, come Cégeste! You must get used to following me.*

Cégeste steps from the mirror, a metal valise in his hand.

PRINCESS: *Will you close the doors.*

CÉGESTE: *What doors?*

PRINCESS: *The mirror. You will never understand what's said to you.*

Cégeste closes the two sides of the mirror. The Princess and Cégeste move toward the bed, where Heurtebise has drawn himself up stiffly, as if at attention.

PRINCESS: *Greetings!*

HEURTEBISE: *Greetings!*

PRINCESS: *Is everything all right?*

HEURTEBISE: *That depends.*

PRINCESS: *What do you mean by that?*

HEURTEBISE: *Nothing, Madame.*

PRINCESS: *So much the better. Should one revolt, I would be supremely displeased.*

The Princess turns and moves toward Cégeste as the latter is closing the trapdoor.

PRINCESS (as she walks): *Orpheus is in the garage?*

HEURTEBISE: *Yes, Madame.*

PRINCESS: *Well, Cégeste, why are you making such a face? Doubtless you expected to see me work with a shroud and scythe. But, my boy, if I were to appear to the living as they picture me, they would recognize me, and that would not facilitate our task.*

Cégeste moves to the table.

PRINCESS: *Heurtebise will help you. You'll never finish. I will close the drapes myself, since neither of you thought of it.* (She closes them.) *Leave nothing on the table but the transmitter.*

Penumbra.

PRINCESS: *Cégeste, send the messages. Come, come, snap out of it. It has done you no good to have stopped drinking. I don't have time to waste.*

(Light radiated by the Princess.) Cégeste stands before the table and touches the apparatus; the clatter of the transmission key is heard.

CÉGESTE (voice of the messages): *The little widows' crepe is really too good to last. Twice. The little widows' crepe is really too good to last. Twice. I repeat: the little widows' crepe . . .*

PRINCESS (moving toward Cégeste, ironically): *Your phrases are absolutely exquisite inventions. Where are my gloves?*

HEURTEBISE: *They're not in the bag.*

The phrases continue, and the figures R. R. 7. 2. 3. 7. 3. 5. 5. 7. 12. I repeat (etc.) and telegraph.

PRINCESS (to Cégeste): *Could you have forgotten them? That would be the limit!*

CÉGESTE: *Yes, Madame. Madame must forgive me.*

PRINCESS: *I knew it. Give me yours.*

Cégeste passes her his rubber gloves.

PRINCESS: *Quick . . . quick . . . To your post. You know that I insist on meticulous discipline, as on board a ship.*

The Princess circles the bed as she finishes putting on the gloves. Eurydice lies there, inanimate, lighted by the fitful luminosity of Cégeste's apparatus.

HEURTEBISE: *Do you have any orders?*

The Princess straightens and removes the gloves.

PRINCESS: *What did you say?*

HEURTEBISE: *I asked if you have orders.*

PRINCESS: *When I execute the orders given to me, I insist that others execute my orders.*

HEURTEBISE: *That's precisely why I ask if you have orders.*

PRINCESS: *How dare you!*

HEURTEBISE: *If you had orders, your killers would have finished the job.*

PRINCESS: *Could it be that you are in love with this idiot?*

HEURTEBISE: *And if I am?*

PRINCESS: *You're not free to love either in one world or in the other.*

HEURTEBISE: *Nor are you.*

The Princess, enraged, advances on Heurtebise.

PRINCESS: *What?*

HEURTEBISE: *One cannot escape the rules.*

The two characters confront each other (profile against profile).

PRINCESS: *I order you to be silent!*

HEURTEBISE: *You're in love with Orpheus and you don't know what to do about it.* . . .

PRINCESS: *Silence!* (Her dress turns white.) She exits off camera.

HEURTEBISE: *I* . . . (angry gesture).

He disappears on the spot. The Princess rushes toward Cégeste's table. Her robe becomes black again.

PRINCESS: *Send your messages! Send your messages! Invent something, anything.*

CÉGESTE (facing into the room): *Madame . . . would I be able to disappear and appear like Heurtebise?*

PRINCESS: *You're too clumsy! Transmit!*

CÉGESTE (radio voice). *Jupiter enlightens those he wishes to confuse. I repeat. Jupiter* . . .

In the garage. The camera frames Orpheus' face close to the radio, his hand on the dials. We hear the end of the preceding phrase:

RADIO: *Jupiter enlightens those he wishes to confuse. Three times. Jupiter enlightens those he wishes to confuse. Attention, listen* (telegraph) . . . (The text continues during the dialogue.) *The night sky is a May hedge.* . . .

The camera focuses on Heurtebise in the doorway.

HEURTEBISE: *Orpheus! Orpheus!*

ORPHEUS: *Won't anyone ever leave me alone!*

The camera shows Orpheus sitting inside the car, turned toward Heurtebise, who is standing in the doorway.

HEURTEBISE: *Your wife is in great danger. Follow me.*

RADIO: *The night sky is a May hedge. I repeat: The night sky* (etc.).

ORPHEUS: *Shut up!* . . . (He seizes his papers and writes with them propped against his knee.)

HEURTEBISE: *I tell you that your wife is in grave danger.*

ORPHEUS: *You keep me from hearing* . . .

HEURTEBISE: *Are you listening to me?*

ORPHEUS: *Wait 'til I finish writing* (he writes . . .) "*May hedge* . . ."

HEURTEBISE (screaming): *Orpheus, your wife is dying!*

ORPHEUS: *You don't know her. Those are just acts she puts on to make me come back to the house.*

Heurtebise exits off camera. The camera frames the whole of Eurydice's bed and the Princess standing near her. Head of the bed. The princess finishes removing a metal band from Eurydice's neck. Eurydice will speak as Cégeste spoke in the chalet scene (flat voice).

PRINCESS: *Rise.*

Eurydice is made to rise by the process of running the film backward. She steps out of bed and finds herself standing face to face with the Princess.

PRINCESS: *You know who I am.*

EURYDICE: *Yes.*

PRINCESS: *Say it.*

The camera frames the trapdoor as it opens. Heurtebise lifts the door and remains at the head of the steps. While the camera rests on this image, we hear the rest of the dialogue.

VOICE OF EURYDICE: *My death.*

VOICE OF THE PRINCESS: *You belong henceforth to the other world.*

EURYDICE: *I belong henceforth to the other world.*

PRINCESS: *You will obey my orders.*

EURYDICE: *I will obey.*

PRINCESS: *Perfect.* (To Heurtebise) *Ah! So there you are. Orpheus must have refused to follow you.*

HEURTEBISE: *I'll speak . . . elsewhere.*

PRINCESS: *And I'll speak too. I have a great deal to say about it.*

The princess passes in front of Eurydice, who stands immobile, a little in front of the foot of the bed. She moves toward Cégeste as she removes her gloves, tossing them on Orpheus' bed. Close-up of the rubber gloves falling on Orpheus' bed. The Princess concludes the movement leading her to Cégeste, who is hastily cleaning up and closing the valise.

PRINCESS: *Don't forget your paraphernalia. You always forget everything! . . .*

Cégeste packs and closes the valise.

PRINCESS: *Good.* (She turns to Heurtebise). *I suppose, Heurtebise, that you want to remain on earth. In the opening of that trapdoor you really do look like a gravedigger. You're quite ridiculous.*

HEURTEBISE: *I'm not the only one.*

PRINCESS: *I have noted your insolence. Cégeste!*

Cégeste loiters next to the bed, and seems astonished to see two Eurydices. One on the bed, the other walking toward the Princess.

PRINCESS: *Teach yourself never to look behind you. There are those who turn themselves into pillars of salt by that little game.*

She shatters the mirror with a blow of her fist. The mirror collapses. Her dress becomes white. The procession enters into the broken mirror. The mirror silently recomposes itself. Heurtebise approaches the reconstituted mirror that reflects his image. He turns. As reflected in the mirror, we see him move toward the bed upon which Eurydice is stretched out. Close-up of the dead Eurydice. The hand of Heurtebise rests on her forehead.

Seen downward from the bedroom window: In front of the garage Orpheus exits; he seems to close the door with regret.

HEURTEBISE: (from the window): *Orpheus! I warned you. You come too late. . . . .*

ORPHEUS: *Too late?*

VOICE OF HEURTEBISE: *Come up.*

ORPHEUS: *What are you doing in my bedroom?*

HEURTEBISE: *Come in . . . through this window that serves you so well as an exit.*

Orpheus clambers up the ladder. Bedroom. He climbs over the windowsill, and closes the window.

ORPHEUS: *I asked you what you were doing in my bedroom.*

HEURTEBISE: *Your wife . . .*

ORPHEUS: *What about my wife?*

HEURTEBISE: *Your wife is dead.*

ORPHEUS: *You must be joking.*

HEURTEBISE: *That would be an odd sort of joke. You wouldn't listen to me. . . .*

ORPHEUS: (shrieking): *Eurydice! Eurydice!*

HEURTEBISE: *Listen to me . . . listen to me, Orpheus.*

Orpheus throws himself on his knees next to the bed.

ORPHEUS: *Eurydice!*

HEURTEBISE: *It's too late to pity her.*

ORPHEUS (turning toward Heurtebise, his face full of horror and shock): *But how? How? Why?*

HEURTEBISE: *She had a bad fall, and I suspect there is yet another reason. . . .*

ORPHEUS: *But what? What?* (He turns back to Eurydice): *Eurydice! Eurydice! It's not possible! Look at me! Speak to me!*

HEURTEBISE: *There is one way left for you to redeem your folly.*

Close-up of Orpheus twisting his head on the sheets.

ORPHEUS: *It is the dream that continues! My nightmare continues! I must wake up! Wake me up!*

Heurtebise grabs him by the shoulders.

HEURTEBISE: *Listen to me. Will you listen to me? Will you listen to me? . . . Orpheus!*

ORPHEUS (lifting his face): *Everything is useless!*

HEURTEBISE: *There's still a chance.*

ORPHEUS (bitterly): *What is it?*

Heurtebise lifts him with all his strength and forces him to stand up.

HEURTEBISE: *Orpheus!* (shaking him). *Orpheus! . . . You know Death.*

ORPHEUS: *I have spoken of her. I've dreamed of her. I've sung of her. I believed I knew her. I didn't know her. . . .*

HEURTEBISE: *You do know her . . . personally.*

ORPHEUS: *Personally?*

HEURTEBISE: *You've been to her house.*

ORPHEUS: *Her house?*

HEURTEBISE: *In her own room . . .*

ORPHEUS (cry): *The Princess!*

Heurtebise nods his head Yes.

ORPHEUS: *God!* . . . (He tears himself away from Heurtebise.)

End of Orpheus' movement as he tears himself from Heurtebise's grasp and lunges at the mirror.

ORPHEUS: *The mirror* . . .

Heurtebise approaches Orpheus, facing the mirror.

HEURTEBISE: *I reveal to you the secret of secrets. . . . Mirrors are the doors through which death comes and goes. Besides, look at yourself every day of your life in a mirror, and you will see death at work like bees in a glass hive.*

Orpheus passes by him and touches the mirror. He turns back toward Heurtebise.

ORPHEUS: *How do you know these terrible things?*

HEURTEBISE: *Don't be naïve. One couldn't be the kind of chauffeur I am without learning certain . . . terrible things.*

ORPHEUS: *Heurtebise! Nothing can be done.*

HEURTEBISE: *Join her.*

ORPHEUS: *No man can do that . . . unless he kills himself.*

HEURTEBISE: *A poet is more than a mere man.*

ORPHEUS: *But my wife is there . . . dead . . . on her deathbed!* . . .

As reflected in the mirror, he turns and throws himself on the head of the bed.

HEURTEBISE: *It is one of her forms, just as the Princess is one of the forms of Death. All that is false. Your wife dwells in another world into which I invite you to follow me.*

ORPHEUS: *I would follow her into Hell.* . .

HEURTEBISE: *No one asks that much of you.*

ORPHEUS: *Heurtebise . . . I want to join Eurydice.*

HEURTEBISE: *You don't have to beg me. I offer her to you* (placing his hands on Orpheus' shoulders). *Orpheus, look me in the eye. Is it Eurydice you wish to join, or Death?*

ORPHEUS: *But . . .*

HEURTEBISE: *Don't forget, I am asking you a specific question. Is it Death you wish to find, or Eurydice?*

ORPHEUS (dropping his gaze): *Both . . .*

HEURTEBISE: *. . . And if possible, to betray one with the other . . .*

ORPHEUS (throwing himself toward the mirror): *We must hurry.*

HEURTEBISE: *I congratulate myself on no longer being in this life.*

The camera focuses on Orpheus' bed where lie the gloves forgotten by his Death. Heurtebise's hand enters the field of vision, and removes them from view.

HEURTEBISE: *Someone left their gloves here.*

ORPHEUS: *Gloves?*

HEURTEBISE: *Put them on. . . . Come on, come on . . . put them on.* (He tosses them to Orpheus.)

Orpheus catches the gloves. He hesitates a moment, then puts them on. (Reverse image.)

HEURTEBISE (next to the mirror): *With these gloves you will go through mirrors as if they were water!*

ORPHEUS: *Prove it to me.*

HEURTEBISE: *Try it. I'll go with you. Look at the time.*

Close-up of the clock, which shows one second to six. Orpheus prepares to enter the mirror, his hands at his sides.

HEURTEBISE: *Hands first!*

Close-up of the gloved hands advancing toward the mirror. We see Orpheus advancing in the mirror. The four hands meet. Seen from the air.

HEURTEBISE: *Are you afraid?*

ORPHEUS: *No, but this mirror is a mirror, and in it I see an unhappy man.*

HEURTEBISE: *It's not necessary to understand. You must believe.*

Orpheus, hands outstretched, enters the mirror. Close-up of the hands as they penetrate the mirror. (Done in a vat of mercury.) In the mirror we see a hazy image of the Zone into which Orpheus and his guide plunge.

Orpheus: **François Périer, Jean Marais, and Marie Déa.**   *Discina*

Then the reflection of the bedroom is re-formed on the surface of the mirror. Iron gate of Orpheus' garden at which the mailman is ringing. He rings a second time, looks around, then slips a letter through the vent in the mailbox. Through the glass partition we see the letter as it slips into the vent.

The Zone. Music.

A street in ruins, resembling some Pompei of Gradiva or some street in a demolished quarter on the Left Bank. A silent wind touches only Heurtebise.

ORPHEUS (walking behind Heurtebise, who advances immobile): *Where are we?*

HEURTEBISE: *Life is long in dying. This is the Zone. It is made of the memories of men and of the ruins of their ways.*

ORPHEUS: *And all the mirrors in the world lead to this Zone?*

HEURTEBISE: *I suppose so, but I wouldn't want to swear to it. Don't think that I know very much more about it than you.*

Orpheus stops, glances around and behind him, which separates him from Heurtebise, who doesn't seem to move, but the Zone rolls by behind him.

HEURTEBISE (turning toward Orpheus without slowing his immobile advance): *Keep walking. . . . Keep walking. . . .*

ORPHEUS (walking and almost catching up to him): *I can hardly keep up with you. You seem to walk without moving. . . .*

HEURTEBISE: *For me it's quite a different matter.*

A glazier crosses the road behind Orpheus.

GLAZIER: *Glazier! Glazier!*

ORPHEUS: *What are they doing, these men who prowl about? Are they alive?*

HEURTEBISE: *They think so. Nothing is more tenacious than professional habit.*

ORPHEUS: *Are we going far?*

HEURTEBISE: *The words you use have no sense in our world.*

ORPHEUS: *There is no wind. Why do you seem to be moving against a wind?*

HEURTEBISE: *Why . . . always why. Don't ask me any more questions, just keep moving. Must I take you by the hand?*

Following a final immobile glissade, Heurtebise clasps Orpheus' hand and drags him along. They cross an esplanade. Next we see them descend a flight of steps and move off to the left against a background of rubbish. The mirrored room in Death's chalet. Behind the table, three judges. At the end of the table, on the right, the court stenographer. Standing in front of the table is Cégeste, dressed as he was at the opening of the film. One of the motorcyclists guards the doorway that opens at the head of the stairs. Closed shutters. Night. Very hard light of the electric lamp on the table and the ceiling. Papers on the table.

TESTAMENT OF ORPHEUS

The Poet Before His Judges

Stage set: A door and steps set in a void. The poet and Cégeste leave the small yard on a satyr. Then they descend the several steps constructed in the void. They cross the threshold of the open door as if it were the end of a corridor.

Only the poet advances toward the table. The thunderclap of a machine breaking the sound barrier is heard. Immediately, in a direct cut, numerous old papers appear on the table and, behind the table, the Princess of *Orpheus* and Heurtebise appear, both simply clad in black like the judges in *Orpheus.*

When the camera has finished moving in on them and stops, they turn toward the poet.

Cégeste, on the appearance of the judges, sits down on a chair apart, near the steps.

POET (who recognizes them): *Well!*

PRINCESS: *Well, what?*

POET: *I beg your pardon. I must have been deceived by an extraordinary resemblance. . . . What are you doing here?*

PRINCESS: *I ask the questions.* (She consults some papers.) *We are the commission of enquiry for a tribunal before which you will be required to account for certain of your actions. This tribunal would like to know if you plead guilty or not guilty.*

(To Heurtebise): *Would you please read the two counts of indictment.*

HEURTEBISE (standing to read): *Primo—You are accused of innocence, which is to say an offense against justice, by being capable and culpable of all crimes rather than of a single crime apt to fall beneath a precise punishment of our jurisdiction.*

Secundo: You are accused of forever wanting to penetrate fraudulently into a world which is not your own. Do you plead guilty or not guilty?

POET: *I plead guilty to the first and second counts. I admit to being hemmed in by the menace of errors I have not committed, and I admit that I have often desired to leap over the fourth mysterious wall on which men write their loves and their dreams.*

PRINCESS: *Why?*

POET: *Doubtless due to fatigue with the world I inhabit and a horror of habit. Also by reason of the disobedience that audacity opposes to rules and of that creative spirit which is the highest form of the spirit of contradiction inherent in men.*

The Princess and Heurtebise exchange a long look.

PRINCESS: *Unless I am mistaken, you make a priesthood of disobedience?*

POET: *Without it what would become of the children, the artists, the heroes?*

HEURTEBISE: *They would count their lucky stars.*

PRINCESS: *We are not here to listen to oratorical jousts. Put that flower on the table.*

The poet places the flower on the table, from which it disappears.

PRINCESS: *Where did you obtain this flower?*

POET: *It was given to me by Cégeste.*

HEURTEBISE: .*Cégeste . . . If I'm not mistaken that is the name of a Sicilian temple?*

POET: *It's also the name of the young poet in my film* Orpheus. *First of all it was the name of the angels in my poem* L'Ange Heurtebise.

The Princess and Heurtebise exchange a long look.

PRINCESS: *What do you understand 'film' to mean?*

POET: *A film is a petrifying source of thought. A film resuscitates dead actions. A film permits one to give the appearance of reality to the irreal.*

PRINCESS: *What do you call the irreal?*

POET: *That which projects beyond our poor limits.*

HEURTEBISE: *In sum, according to you, there would exist individuals like a sleeping invalid, with neither arms nor legs, who dreams that he runs and gestures.*

POET: *You have given there an excellent definition of the poet.*

PRINCESS: *What do you mean by 'poet'?*

POET: *The poet, in composing poems, makes use of a language, neither living nor dead, which few people speak and few understand.*

PRINCESS: *And why do these persons speak this language?*

POET: *In order to meet their compatriots in a world where too often that exhibitionism which consists in displaying one's soul utterly naked is practiced only by blind men.*

HEURTEBISE (beckoning to Cégeste to approach): *Cégeste.*

CÉGESTE: *Present.*

PRINCESS: *Who are you?*

CÉGESTE: *The adopted son of this man. My real name is Edouard. I am a painter.*

PRINCESS: *He calls you a poet under the name of Cégeste.*

HEURTEBISE: *Would Cégeste be your nickname?*

POET: *A pseudonym would be more accurate.*

HEURTEBISE: *Your French is quite subtle.*

PRINCESS (lighting a cigarette under the amused eye of Heurtebise): *Who gave you the right to appear to this man and to bring him this flower?*

CÉGESTE: *This flower was dead. I had received orders to deliver it to him that he might bring it back to life.*

PRINCESS: *Can you furnish me with proof of your powers?*

HEURTEBISE: *And don't think that just disappearing will be enough to convince us.*

POET: *Disappearing, however, is not convenient.*

HEURTEBISE: *No more so than the phenomenon that obliges men who love to obliterate themselves before the object of their love.*

PRINCESS (striking the table): *Have you lost your head!*

HEURTEBISE: *I beg your pardon. I, too, am occasionally distracted.*

PRINCESS: *I advise you not to jest stupidly and awkwardly about things that might risk enlightening men as to the vanity of their enterprises.*

HEURTEBISE: *As yet there's nothing to fear on that score* (to Cégeste). *You were asked to furnish proof of your powers.*

CÉGESTE (designating the Poet): *I share the opinion of that man that everything provable is vulgar. You must, alas! take my word for it.*

PRINCESS (icily): *Would you dare to give me lessons? That would be the end. I have noted it well.* (Turns to the poet.) *Sir!*

The Poet, who has been staring fixedly at Heurtebise, turns his eyes toward the Princess.

POET: *I'm listening.*

PRINCESS: *Did you write:*

> This body that contains us knows not our own
> What inhabits us is yet inhabited
> And these bodies, ones in others,
> Are the body of eternity.

POET: *I admit to having written it.*

PRINCESS: *And from whom did you get such things?*

POET: *What things?*

PRINCESS: *The things you speak in this language neither living nor dead.*

POET: *From no one.*

PRINCESS (violently): *You lie!*

POET: *I'll grant you that if you admit as I do that we are the servants of an unknown force that lives within us, manipulates us, and dictates to us this language.*

HEURTEBISE (leaning toward the Princess): *It's not impossible that he may be an idiot. . . .*

PRINCESS: *Intellectuals are less to be feared.*

POET: *Mascarille and Leporello passed for their masters. Poets resemble them a bit.*

PRINCESS: *Cease your babbling. Do not speak unless I address you.*

POET: *I was explaining myself in all humility.*

HEURTEBISE: *You are not asked to be either humble or proud. You are asked to reply when questioned. One point, that's all. Do not forget that you are a nocturnal amalgam of caverns, forests, swamps, red torrents, amalgam populated by fabulous and gigantic beasts that devour each other. It's nothing to talk so big about.*

The Princess places her hand on Heurtebise's arm to recall him to order.

PRINCESS (annoyed): *Please bring forward the witness.*

In a lap dissolve the professor appears before the table in his pajamas.

PROFESSOR (as if abruptly awakened): *Where am I?*

HEURTEBISE: *Professor, that is a phrase unworthy of a man of science. It's the phrase of a pretty woman who pretends she has fainted and is just coming to.*

PROFESSOR: *I was in bed. . . . I was sleeping. . . .*

PRINCESS: *You are in bed, Professor, and you are sleeping. Only, you are not dreaming. You occupy one of those folds in time that you have made the object of study—study that honors your intelligence but of which our reign scarcely approves. You will awake and remember us as if we were characters in your dream.* (Pointing to the poet.) *Do you know this man?*

The Professor dons his glasses and regards the Poet. He hesitates.

POET: *Professor! You have a short memory. True, your excuse is that you're asleep. Didn't you recently strip me of my Louis XV chrysalis: cape, boots, jabot, white wig, tricornered hat, riding whip.*

PROFESSOR (jovial): *Why, of course!*

POET: *I reproach you for nothing. You had honestly forewarned me that you were not very coherent.*

PROFESSOR: *And what are you doing here?*

PRINCESS (annoyed): *I repeat to you, gentlemen, that I command here. I will thank you to keep silent and to answer only to my questions.* (To the Professor): *Under what circumstances did you meet this man?*

PROFESSOR: *It's quite simple. . . .*

POET (smiling): *That's one point of view.*

HEURTEBISE: *Silence!*

PRINCESS: *Answer!*

PROFESSOR: *I despaired of bringing to light the considerable discovery of a resurrectional method, and it is probable that my discovery would have died with me, if this man—endowed with powers of which I am ignorant, had not left our continuum, voyaged in the intemporal, lost himself in it, and had not brought back from my future into my present the proof of my later success. I made the experiment on him. I should add that, for fear of losing the esteem of my colleagues at the Institute, I threw my discovery out the window into the Seine . . . the river that flows before my house.*

PRINCESS: *You might thus have accomplished the tour de force of returning to his own era a man lost in time?*

PROFESSOR: *Just barely. I rescued him from a pit into which his dangerous attempt had caused him to fall.*

POET: *Only causing me to fall into another abyss, Professor. For I do not call a return to life the dusk, the sort of twilight through which I have wandered since leaving your laboratory.*

PROFESSOR: *That I deplore. It is, alas, possible that my discovery was not absolutely perfected. I am all the happier that I destroyed it.*

HEURTEBISE: *What form did it take, this discovery?*

PROFESSOR: *A box of balls which my powder propulsed faster than the speed of light. The box is what I threw into the river.*

HEURTEBISE: *Let us hope that there are no disagreeable mutations as a result. In any event, it was the wisest move.*

PRINCESS: *In so pridefully disorganizing measures (though awkward) interpreted by your world as its original disorder, men strongly risk breaking a chain to give themselves the illusion of progress.*

PROFESSOR: *Madame! By that statement you condemn all science.*

HEURTEBISE: *What you call science. For there is also a science of the soul with which mankind concerns itself exceedingly little.*

The Princess strikes the table and looks at Heurtebise severely.

PRINCESS: *Once again, I must insist . . .*

HEURTEBISE (bowing slightly): *I beg your pardon.*

PRINCESS (to the Professor): *What would you tell me if you had to defend this man?*

PROFESSOR: *That he is a poet, which is to say, he is indispensable, though I don't know to what.*

POET: *Where did you learn that, Professor? Might you be a sorcerer?*

PROFESSOR: *The devil, be careful! Sorcerers are still burned . . . with anxiety. No, it is simply parapsychology. Scientists are not always as limited as certain creative artists might suppose. May I, Madame, ask you a question in turn?*

PRINCESS: *We'll see if I'm at liberty to answer you.*

PROFESSOR: *The simple curiosity of a man of science. Here you are: What time is it?*

HEURTEBISE: *No time, Professor. None. Continue to sleep. You are free.*

PROFESSOR (rather vaguely): *Thank you. I feel . . . a sort of difficulty of being . . . a manner of fatigue . . . It seems to me . . .*

HEURTEBISE (kindly): *Sleep. Sleep, Professor. I will it.*

PROFESSOR: *Thank you . . . Madame . . . my respects . . .* (he removes his glasses and in a faraway voice): *I sleep.*

He disappears in a lap dissolve.

PRINCESS (to the Poet): *I am well aware that the meanderings of your itinerary form a sort of labyrinth far removed from our own, even though the paths cross, and that if it has been possible for you to discover the single person apt to correct your errors and your disobedience of terrestial laws, this act benefited, not from a distraction of the unknown, but from a sort of supreme indulgence which it happens you have, dear sir, abused and which might very well be withdrawn from you one day. If I overstep my prerogatives here, it is only because I insisted on warning you, before inquiring of your guide the limits of his privileges and responsibilities.*

POET: *I have difficulty understanding you.*

HEURTEBISE: *No one is asking you to understand.*

PRINCESS: *Don't play village idiots. It seems to me that you understand perfectly and that you have chosen to play the imbecile rather than to confess.*

POET: *But Madame . . .*

HEURTEBISE: *You ought to congratulate yourself on the incredible forbearance the preventative tribunal has exhibited in your case.*

PRINCESS (gesturing toward Cégeste): *Step forward.* (Cégeste hesitates.) *Yes . . . you . . . you . . .*

Cégeste approaches the table.

PRINCESS: *Are you quite certain that you have not sheered off from your own chief in order to fuse the personalities that divide you and because it disturbs you to be of a dual nature? Were you not tempted to form them into a single personality in service to the extravagances of this man, also a duality: your father, actual and adoptive?*

CÉGESTE: *Madame, you must surely be conversant in the terrible infinity of reigns and orders that often prevent an understanding of which persons ought to obey and which ought to be obeyed.*

The Princess and Heurtebise lean toward each other and confer in low voices.

PRINCESS (to the Poet): *Do you consider it necessary to add something else in your defense?*

POET: *I have to say that if I merit a punishment, I could not conceivably suffer one more painful than that which obliges me to dwell between two realities, or, to employ your language, between two kingdoms.*

A filmmaker would say: "in false color." I would give much to tread on firm earth once more and not to be lost in the penumbra of a strange universe.

PRINCESS: *That is scarcely within our province. The tribunal will judge.* (She gathers together the papers on the table, and rises.) *The commission of inquiry preventatively condemns you to the pain of life.*

The Princess disappears in a fade.

HEURTEBISE: *The minimum. Especially at your age.* (He brings forth from behind his back the flower that he had been hiding in his right hand.) *Your flower . . .*

POET (very low): *Heurtebise!*

HEURTEBISE (a finger against his lips): *Shhh!*

POET (still low): *And the Princess?*

HEURTEBISE: *You know full well that she dared, caught by a mortal, transgress the laws of the time of men.*

POET: *And Orpheus?*

HEURTEBISE: *His survival was a mirage. His divine head is dead, and Eurydice has returned to hell. A great human voice once said: "Never spit against the wind." Take your flower.*

POET: *I dare not take it.*

HEURTEBISE: *This is neither the first nor the last time that I take this flower from you, only to return it.*

POET: *I have some recognition of the courage of your gesture and that I risk subjecting you to condemnation once again. Her and you . . .*

HEURTEBISE: *We cannot be condemned to a worse fate.*

POET: *To what, then, have they condemned you?*

HEURTEBISE (gravely, slowly): *To judge others. To be the judges.*

He disappears in a very slow dissolve.

CRITICAL SPECTRUM

> *Not everyone is able to follow in*
> *the footsteps of such a bard. In all*
> *his films, Jean Cocteau tirelessly*
> *proves to us that in order to know*
> *how to create cinema we must re-*
> *turn to Méliès, and for this a good*
> *number of years of Lumière are*
> *still before us.*
>
> —JEAN-LUC GODARD

DICTIONNAIRE DES METTEURS EN SCÈNE FRANÇAIS

He constructs tables, and it is up to others to make them sing. "I am a draftsman," he says; "it is natural for me to see and hear what I write, to endow it with a plastic form." Let us translate: He is a poet. A poet gifted for the cinema, and thus a great filmmaker. It is a fact that all his films, including *L'Aigle à deux têtes,* a flamboyant and moving film, wrongly underestimated, are admirable. Anxious to transcend mere decorative art, he sometimes achieves a realism, a rawness almost obscene (*Les Parents terribles*). His dialogues, despite their theatrical emphasis and poetic heaviness, ring truer than anything we've heard in the so-called realist or psychological films. As one of his characters says, we are with him "in legend, right up to our necks." The sparkling and excruciating *Orpheus* is like a prism through which are diffused all the nets of light from a particularly shimmering and richly dispersed thought. It's not surprising that this prism sparkles like a diamond. Realism and dream (". . . with the air of living, but living a storybook life," he commented of the characters in *Beauty and the Beast*) are joined by him in a sort of cinema once removed that he was capable of materializing—a friendly artisan who knows the value of the hand and of the "worker"—with an exemplary boldness and courage. Deprived of him for seven years, French cinema has not accepted the inevitable and limps along cast down.

(*Cahiers du Cinéma,* No. 17, May, 1957)

ANDRÉ BAZIN

Theatre Transformed by Black-and-White Magic into Pure Cinema

Cocteau, who before the war had contemplated an adaptation [of *Les Parents terribles*] substantially modifying the play, finally opted for a paradoxical solution: he changed nothing of the text and very little of the setting. The play, I mean the film, practically takes place in three acts: "The Caravan," "Madeleine's Apartment," "The Caravan." We never leave this framework that could easily fit between the footlights, the wings, and the backdrop of a theatre. At the very most, the theatre bedroom has taken on the dimensions of a small apartment. But we are carefully kept from leaving it, even if the characters do. When the inhabitants of the chock-full caravan cross Paris to visit Madeleine, we find them in the hall before the door. The exterior world—the street—is evoked but once, by the siren of a fire engine. Even this noise could be theatrical sound effects.

What we must now attempt to explain is why, in taking what is apparently the least possible cinematographic tack, Cocteau made *Les Parents terribles* one of the purest morsels of cinema of these last ten years.

Let us first make the circumstances clear. The enterprise was served by an exceptional conjuncture. With the exception of one actress: Josette Day (who is precisely the only one who does not act in unison), one may say that every frame of this film had been rehearsed, on stage, more than a thousand times. The actors had reached the point at which the habit of the role creates a second nature for them. One senses that they are capable of shedding real tears ten times in a row before the camera, if necessary, to perfect a retake. They evolve in their sentiments and in their universe with as much ease and security as you take your subway. If one adds, as Cocteau took pleasure in repeating, that, half by coincidence and half by identification with their respective roles, each of them felt lifelike in his role (to the point that scenes sometimes prolonged themselves backstage), one grasps the extraordinary homogeneity of the acting. It is extremely rare in cinema that an interpretation imposes itself through style. In *Les Parents terribles,* however diverse their talents, all the actors play in perfect harmony. One senses that it would be easier for them to act falsely than not to act in this spirit that unites them like an old conspiracy. The habitual conditions of the film studio, the slow, piecemeal work, the absence of an audience, do not allow them to maintain the intense warmth that remains ordinarily the privilege of a stage performance.

I believe, too, that it is the hundreds of stage rehearsals that enabled Cocteau so triumphantly to win his directing long shot. So frequently polished by contact with an audience, the play had attained its precise dramatic patina, and Cocteau knew all its contours as the hand of a blind man knows those of a familiar object. At every moment, to any given word and any given gesture, Cocteau could direct the attention and emotion of a spectator. He ignored no detail of the real and imaginary script that is the fruit of attention and emotion, and of which cinematographic editing is in large part nothing more than a plastic transcription. If I discuss at length the conditions presiding over the shooting of this film, it is certainly not with the intention of diminishing the merits of Cocteau, but to underscore, as he did himself, the privileged character of such a success, and to guard us from the temptation of believing that it could easily be repeated.

Having said this, we have yet to come to the secret of the film, to the black-and-white magic that, without having changed its appearance, transformed this block of theatre into pure cinema.

Did Cocteau reveal this secret to us in saying that he had conceived his film in 16 mm., that is, using his camera with the ideal mobility and liberty of a hand camera? I don't think that this whim, although it is illuminating with regard to the conception behind the technical scripting, can explain the essential reasons for our pleasure. It is true that *Les*

Parents terribles marks an important date in the history of film scripting. In spite of the relatively large number of sequences, of the startling liberty of shots and angles, one would say that whole scenes consist of a single sequence, so much do numberless cuts go unperceived. It would be illusory merely to put this down to an exceptionally steady hand; the extraordinary impression of infallible continuity that links the images is not due solely to supple and flexible editing. It has a reason both psychological and esthetic. One might doubtless define it this way: Whatever may be the point of view from which the camera approaches the action, the camera never abandons its role of witness, of spectator. One might say that *Les Parents terribles* is the reverse of the pseudosubjective camera in *Lady in the Lake*.[1] In all film, the director treats us alternately as spectators of and as characters in the drama; sometimes he asks us to watch and sometimes to participate (the majority of close-ups of objects, for example, identify us with the actor who is upset by or interested in that object). Yet is not one of the essential characteristics of the theatre precisely that it is impossible to be other than spectator to it? Therefore it is certainly not because he leads us among his characters, occasionally giving us the most unexpected images of them, that Cocteau ceases to create theatre. He makes use of this liberty, which only the cinema could give him, to deepen and confirm us in the role of spectators. In this supertheatre of the screen, there is not a single shot in which we are allowed to escape our position as witnesses. From beginning to end, impotent and curious, we are condemned to watch. And even "watch" is hardly an accurate description. For Cocteau treats the camera like a keyhole through which he spies on the action and the actors. We are obliged to share his indiscretion. Hence the strange tension of this spectacle in which the most ordinary incident always seems to have an indefinable air of indecency, as of an intimacy surprised. In the theatre we were merely spectators; through the cinema Cocteau makes each of us a voyeur.

But this esthetic principle is insufficient to explain the unerring sure-

[1] An American film by Robert Montgomery, in which the camera identifies exclusively with the principal character.—ED.

ness of the choice of shots. If their boldness seems so natural to us, it is because it is always founded on a precise knowledge of our reactions as spectators, as the ideal spectator, variable as a Cartesian diver and curious as the devil. An example? The most audacious shot in the film is taken directly from the stage. This is where Jean Marais confesses to Yvonne de Bray his love for Madeleine. He has placed his head against his mother's and they both look straight into the audience. The camera moves in to frame their faces in such a way that we see no more than Marais's mouth and the eyes of Yvonne de Bray, the remainder of their faces being cut off the edges of the screen. Yet if one thinks about it in recalling the play, it becomes apparent that the actors' position was exactly the same on stage and that the dramatic tension was such that the spectator mentally saw the same close-up: the only things that counted in that moment were

Les Parents terribles: **Yvonne de Bray, Marcel André, and Gabrielle Dorziat.**

Sirius

Mic's mouth and Sophie's eyes. I could multiply such examples, while adding that Cocteau knew how to use the camera to hide as well as to reveal. Every theatre director dreams of being able to force the spectator, when necessary, not to watch the actor who is speaking but to watch his interlocutor. Here this is achieved, thanks to extremely frequent employment of the off-camera voice.

There is still a great deal more to say about this film that poses a thousand questions and answers them by the most unexpected detours. But one must resign oneself to concluding. *Les Parents terribles,* like several other films, including *La Vipère* and, to a certain extent, *Hamlet,* presents a decisive solution to the problem of filmed theatre. We wouldn't risk contending that it is the only possible solution, but the particular interest of this one is demonstrating that a unique fidelity to the spirit and conventions of the theatre is not only compatible with the screen but may even be proof of the greatest cinematographic invention. In truth, if there is such a deal of cinema in *Les Parents terribles*—of the purest kind—it is because Cocteau was determined to put more theatre into it than had existed in the play.

(*L'Ecran français,* 1948)

CHRIS MARKER

The Most Advanced Frontiers of Demiurgy

Orpheus opens to several keys and on several levels. The true public, sensitive, capable of penetrating the film simply by the power of identification inherent in cinema, may fear itself. The initiated, possessor of the first key, who reads in this Orpheus-Cocteau as he read in *The Blood of a Poet* his more explicit condemnation, can no longer identify. The prolongations, the harmonies are denied him. Naïveté, prerequisite for the spectator, is denied him. He sees in this spectacle something that concerns him—to wit: his own responsibility. If there exists in this world a Cocteau legend, a caricature of Cocteau, which makes of this artisan a "man of the world," of this monk a trapeze artist, of his splendor a kind of gaudiness, it is the work of the first-nighters. "The gesturings of a man who treads on Death must appear rather curious," wrote Cocteau in 1923. Since then, if he reveals his game, if this reverse illusionist uncovers his gimmicks, opens his trunks, reveals that his white magic is really black magic, his pigeons alive, his ladies actually cut to bits, and that he truly treads on Death, why then his following dwindles. Superciliously excluded from the debate between Orpheus and his Death, incapable of the humility and detachment through which a simple spectator can nevertheless take his part in the sacrifice, the public loses interest in a dream that ceases to be its own.

. . . . Just as the spectator who laughs at *The Blood of a Poet* is surely forced to see himself in the interior of the film applauding the torture —and consequently to judge himself—here the critic is already made ineffective in advance. When R. S. in *l'Observateur* writes: "In no other film . . . does one cross through the mirror more often. But this time no one believes in it," he only repeats the words of the statue in *Blood:* "I congratulate you. You wrote that one entered mirrors and you didn't believe it." And that's precisely the problem, and Cocteau is perfectly conscious of this division. But this is also the function of the poet, the constant, exhausting effort to reduce the two antithetical faces of reality. It is on this time lag between two worlds that poetry constructs its relief, like a stereoscope. And it is in this that cinematography becomes the best vehicle for poetic exploration. One doesn't cross the mirror. One doesn't cross through the screen. And yet one does cross through the screen, live the lives of the characters, inhabit the world of the screen. The film becomes the extreme outpost, the farthest advanced frontier of demiurgy. That it must appear vulgar, ridiculous according to the lights of a certain nostalgia for poetic intervention in the "real" world, is evident. But one might as well reproach man for not being God. An entirely victorious poetry would be silence, and it is in poetry's failure, in its unsatisfied reaching toward an impossible reconciliation that it overwhelms distance, reducing these beautiful cadavers to the point at which we recognize ourselves.

Perhaps this is why cinema holds this unique position for Jean Cocteau, why it is not by the prestige of a new technique, or of a toy (Welles's "electric train") that he penetrates into his work, but through the ambiguous nature of the world closest to the world, of the last lie before the truth. In his poetic experience in all the arts, Cocteau followed the inverse order of the Hegelian specter who, from architecture to poetry, presents the itinerary of disincarnation. The entire spectrum of Jean Cocteau's work, in contrast, is an effort toward the most exact weighing and comprehension of the world. At first subjugated to orders and messages from the invisible, bound to his receiver like a radio operator, delivering in his poems the transcripts of his interviews like Orpheus in his car, he never stopped seeking—in the novel, in theatre, design, travel, by language, color, the snowy brass of a pipe cleaner or the ink of light—new methods of precipitating the invisible, of trapping Death, an ink that denounces the presence of angels and shows us phantoms suddenly become blue trees. Cinematography is the last and richest of these modes of investigation. We know the importance Cocteau attaches to waves, to signals, to all methods of mechanical revelation. He often represents the poet as a sort of recording mechanism. Doubtless he regards the camera as a machine for multiplying and sharpening the senses, an X-ray lamp that reveals more than what one places before it, a tool for surprising secrets. "The surprises of photography" was a subtitle for *The Blood of a Poet,* in which Cocteau, "trapped by his own film," attributed to the camera's discernment the revelation of his own face in the place of his hero. And we recall the photographer in *Mariés de la Tour Eiffel.* Inverse miracle from that of the scrambling fakir whom the eyes see but the film never registers, Cocteau dreams of a film sufficiently sensitive to delimit precise figures, where the human eye would see nothing but confusion. While waiting, he collaborates with mystery, he offers to the monster camera prepared nourishment, of course, but it is a food from which he ultimately expects a prodigious metamorphosis. Thus he was able to write, as he did concerning *Blood of a Poet:* "Can I blame anyone for misunderstanding a film that I understand so poorly myself?" and detach himself from his film, distant as sleep, untellable as a dream, transmittable only by means of that other miracle of which only the cinematographer is capable: making others dream it.

(*Esprit,* November, 1950)

HENRI AGEL

A Nocturnal Universe

The story of the relationship between Jean Cocteau and the French cinema is one of the most dazzling and satisfactory stories imaginable. In seven years (1943–1950) there is not a single one of the great cinematographic genres that the author of *Clair-Obscur* has not defended and illustrated with a singular brilliance.

This plenitude of creation that, on the screen, has been reserved to so few men and that Cocteau has known three times over, this plenitude is the prolongation (perhaps the culmination) of an already fecund career, consecrated in large part to poetry. That a great poet should have become a great filmmaker is a unique adventure on which one long may muse.

Thus we begin to more closely define the cinematographic universe of Cocteau, and this universe appears to us to be of an essentially nocturnal essence. The tragic in *Les Parents terribles,* which is—as Bazin remarked—the tragedy of cohabitation and claustration, imposes a rarefied air, a physical and intellectual suffocation, resulting in large part from the fact that the strength of aeration and dilation have been crushed by a sort of black destiny. The artificial nature of the work in the studio underscored, by its murderous rigor, this atmosphere; "the least ray of sunlight, any light other than electric would have destroyed this fragile and fatal symbiosis" (A. Bazin). For her part, the reptilian countenance of Yvonne de Bray, having already dominated *The Eternal Return,* imposed this mood of oily shadows that could not help provoking a manifestation of evil. *Les Parents terribles,* an integration of the tragedy of antiquity into the coordinates of the boulevards of Paris, is truly "a voyage to the end of night" with the caravan dwellers. Could one not say of *Beauty and the Beast* and of *Orpheus* that they are also grand nocturnal expeditions?

The fairy tale of Mme. Leprince de Beaumont has become the transcription of the eternal antagonism confronting the diurnal powers—the world of Avenant, of the merchant, and of his daughters and son—and the powers of night, crystallized in the Beast's domain. Beauty, mediator between light and darkness, must plunge into the depths of this subterranean kingdom, confront its marvels and monsters, in order to extract from its Dionysiac matrix the pure Apollonian diamond—the same diving bell to the unfathomable center of the world described in *Orpheus*. The same descent into the infraworld, in the midst of squalls and ruins, the same vertigo on the threshold of this "abyss forbidden to our probings." Here the itinerary is the same as it was twenty years ago, and takes up the spoor of *The Blood of a Poet*. But the black-gloved statue has become the foreign princess, and Maria Casarès reveals the beating of a sensitive heart beneath the folds of her strict uniform of mourning. At the very sources of night, in the most secret heart of death, there is a mystery that had been blinded by the light of day. These themes, which are fragrant and palpable verities to Cocteau, have sketched in all his films the lines of force of a mental universe, plunging resolutely into the most menacing strata of invisibility. . . .

But the salient point is that this determined archaism or primitivism melts itself with the subtlety of the symbolism and the refinements of the texts to form a baroque style—certainly not warm and juice-filled like that of a Blasetti, but willfully funereal and chilly, after the fashion of a monumental triumph of death. We do not believe, in effect, that the baroque style is limited to a frenetic exaltation of the discordant powers of life. It subsumes as well a gloomy liturgy, of which classic and Spanish art have given several handsome examples. It is this high style that Cocteau was able to capture in order to impose the concentrated horror of *Les Parents terribles,* all the more fatal because dissimulated behind a wry grimace.

(*La Table Ronde,* October, 1955)

CLAUDE MAURIAC

Frontal Attack on the Marvelous

Jean Cocteau has always written in congenial ink. A whisper from the poet, and the white pages are covered with signs and designs. What Cocteau called the ink of light, cinematography, is the most mysterious of all these inks.

More than twenty years later, Cocteau attempted to put into effect the method that he had discovered earlier and that consists in the absence of method: that is to say, that the sacrosanct rules of the trade are most often useless hindrances. "There is no film technique," he was able to declare. "There is the technique that everyone discovers for himself": it is the technique that is most closely adaptable to whatever the author intends to express. To the "This is done," "That is not done" of The School, Cocteau responds with an astonishing mockery. One just doesn't switch from a long shot to a close-up. But when you use binoculars at a racetrack, what are you doing? He reminds us of "the marvelous lesson of Charlie Chaplin in *Monsieur Verdoux,* which is a masterpiece of offhandedness vis-à-vis the rules," notably the switch from the tiny craft to the close-up of Monsieur Verdoux rowing. Cocteau himself tells us that *The Blood of a Poet* and, in similar fashion, *Beauty and the Beast,* which, oddly enough, also bears his signature, are aimed at the aficionados: "Of course [in these films] I don't kill the bull according to the rules. But this disdain for rules is not without a disdain for danger that excites a great number of souls."

Jean Cocteau is not *merely* amusing, as some still too often think; he is *also* amusing: it is his recompense and ours. But in the beginning he wrote nothing, for the cinema or anything else, which was not dear to his heart. It is therefore hardly surprising that a childhood episode that had profoundly marked him, that of a schoolboy injured by a snowball, should reappear in diverse forms both in his literary works (notably in a passage in *Les Enfants terribles*) and in *The Blood of a Poet*.[1] This is why his films present such possibilities for exegesis. But if one questions Cocteau about one of them, he often finds it painful to reply, and all the more so because it is possible, he tells us, that "the camera records in advance, around persons and objects, all that man does not discover on his own." Cocteau, the spring-finder, the sorcerer, expects from cinematographic poetry the same revelatory power that he demanded from other modes of poetic expression.

There were numerous trick shots in *The Blood of a Poet,* and they were, for the most part, more subtle than they appear at first glance. The plunge into the mirror, the pulsing heart, the living statue have been discussed. But there were also more secret artifices: eyes painted on Lee Miller's [the statue] eyelids to give her the air of being both there and elsewhere, and the incomprehensible gait of the poet, a sort of disconcerting creep achieved by the actor dragging himself, in reality, along the ground and, after filming the scene on the flat, it was turned right side up.

But, without ever renouncing trick shots (notably in *Orpheus* where he retrieved those of his first film, rendering them even more arresting thanks to advances in technique), Cocteau tried more and more to meet the marvelous face to face. If he is not quite correct in thinking that it is not in the château but rather in the garage of *The Eternal Return* that poetry functions most fully, he is not mistaken in preferring to this other château in *Beauty and the Beast* the episode in the poultry yard with the sedan chair, "a scene which evokes no apparent phantasm"; nor is he mistaken in seeing the black and luxurious automobile of *Orpheus* and his radio as so many ordinary elements, which are nonetheless innovators of the marvelous: "The more one touches on mystery, the more important it becomes to be realistic."

The equilibrium between this sought-for Jansenism of the execution and the flamboyant romanticism of the inspiration was not always as per-

---

[1] This snowball incident also appears in the film of *Les Enfants terribles*—ED.

fect as Jean Cocteau would have wished. So much the better. He who loves "to fly by machine," how could he possibly renounce his dearest vocation in the privileged domain of mechanical fantasy, the cinema? Nevertheless, with *Les Parents terribles* (1949) he obtained from himself a rigor never before achieved. And isn't the fact that his *Orpheus,* just as minutely controlled and devised, but elaborated through antinomic means, was even more successful—is this not proof that Cocteau was right to let himself yield to his temptation, the temptation of magic born of machinery?

(*Petite littérature du Cinéma,* Editions du Cerf, 1957)

JACQUES RIVETTE

Death Taken Seriously

Testament of Orpheus is a poet's film, which is to say it is indispensable, though I don't know to what.[1] But then again I do know: indispensable to our French cinema, which wants not for talented men at the moment, but which wants for this sort of default or lack that is precisely poetry. What is poetry? That which is never out of style, which is linked to neither fashion nor style, but to a poverty turned to riches, a limping turned to dance, in short, to a happy destitution. The poet, above all, must reinvent simplicity, realism, and Cocteau reinvented the documentary, just as Georges Franju, working with Fritz Lang, reinvented the set shot.

Reverse shots, slow motion, apparitions and disappearances with a turn of the crank, recourse to special effects only when necessary for an unforgettable effect: thus is born the art of inventing lasting images.

In a well-known paragraph of "L'Essai de critique indirecte," Cocteau once compared the painter-poet and the poet-painter, Picasso and De Chirico. Filmmaker and poet ever since *L'Aigle à deux têtes,* elegance obliged him, for his own testament, finally to remake himself into the poet and filmmaker of *The Blood of a Poet,* exclusively and unsuccessfully preoccupied with trying to paint roses that are not his self-portrait.

[1] Cocteau had said: "Poetry is indispensable. To what, I don't know. . . ."
—R. G.

But always this Orpheus, always this Oedipus, on the blackboard or the screen, return to flout a false blind man with painted lids, brother of this mask with living eyes that Franju has just unleashed among us.

The artist anxious and reconciled in the same movement. You're quite free to scoff at a treatise on poetic morality, which is to say an analytical and methodical description of the trials, temptations, and resources of the poet, and of why he must always take the word "mortification" in its strictest sense. This desperate effort of men to give meaning to the absurd, which is art, permeates the work of a Ray or a Mizoguchi. Cocteau and Franju seek to storm absurdity in its stronghold, but only to rediscover man behind it all. "Take this flower. . . . But this flower is dead," strange sort of hopscotch, but it causes us to jump suddenly, with both feet— "One cannot always bring back to life the thing that one loves"—into the bull's-eye. For this film is beautiful, in the last analysis, because it is the film of a man who knows that he is going to die and yet is unable, no matter how much he might wish to, to take death seriously. Absurdity and grace are head and tail of the same coin, which he tosses into his night and which falls into our own darkness.

(*Cahiers du Cinéma,* No. 106, April, 1960)

JEAN-LOUIS BORY

A Kind of Metaphorical Confidence

Jean Cocteau did not invent cinema. But—this academy's dictionary, in the preparation of which he participated, will be formal—he invented cinematography. I mean to say that in spite of all difficulties, placing a quasi-Castilian point of honor on this elegantly superannuated coquetry, he adhered to the word. And not only for the pleasure of resisting the flabbiness of vocabulary, but also because the "graphy" of cinematography always signified to him that cinema is a sort of writing capable of venturing into realms where writing per se cannot go. In his own expression, he literally splashed the screen in an "ink of light." A congenial ink, much the same as that which he used for his poems and novels.

As he blotted it, magic appeared.

Magic born of a machine, as in the incredible voyages of Jules Verne. Mirror-machine; an image-capturing machine, a talking machine rendering oracles like Orpheus' horse; a flying machine, crossing through walls, modifying at will the rhythm of time, turning gestures inside out as one tosses a salad. One can well understand that this fabulous "box" fascinated Cocteau and that, very early, before literature had ever thought of accepting cinema into its domain as it had finally accepted the theatre, Cocteau dreamed of putting the camera to work for him.

Which is to say, to work for the poet. Writer of dialogues and scenarios, director, Cocteau continued to do in the cinema what he had done everywhere else: In addition to poetry of the novel, critical poetry, poetry of the theatre, graphic poetry, and poetry-poetry, he "wrote" with reflected light on a screen, cinematographic poetry. The poetry of cinema, which one must be careful not to confuse with poetry in cinema—a ripple photogenically disturbed by a pebble, dewdrops on gossamer, sun swimming in a tropical sea, a wood fire, a rimy pine tree, a scarf of mist. Cocteau hated all this gaudy bazaar—which is precisely what most of the time, alas, both producers and public insist on calling "poetic." For him, cinematographic poetry was first of all a question of style. Visual style, obviously.

Doubtless, Cocteau, for his films, was not always the only captain on board after God, that is, after poetry. Cinema is also industry and commerce. "The heavy burden of millions of francs and time running out" occasionally gave the magician of the darkroom a leaden tread, and perhaps he was only truly free for his first film, *The Blood of a Poet* (1930), and for his last ones, *Orpheus* (1950) and *Testament of Orpheus* (1960). But even excluding this master trilogy, he succeeded in pursuing a sort of metaphorical confidence, slipping in his fixed ideas beneath a thousand and one disguises, both impertinent and grave, practicing rigor beneath tickling, a lightweight for those who judge a book by its cover, "facile" for those who are unaware that the juggler's ease is the result of unending hard work. Suppressing all frontiers between realism and fakery, between the natural and supernatural, even the artificial, Cocteau sounded the depths by multiplying the surfaces: this fake blood, these fake angels, fake mirrors, end by speaking to us of veritable love and true death.

(Arts, October 16, 1963)

WITNESSES: COCTEAU THE MAN

J E A N - P I E R R E   B A S T I D E [1]

Striptease

> *This film is nothing more than a strip-tease show in which my flesh is shed bit by bit, finally revealing my naked soul.*
>
> *September, 1959*

We were twenty years old. In Baux-de-Provence, a film crew was starting on *Testament of Orpheus.* Geneviève had obtained permission to attend the shooting. We had hitchhiked down from Paris to Saint-Rémy, then by foot through the Val d'Enfer. In the village, we were directed to the quarries.

Mourning draperies crackling in the sun on the sill of a balcony marked the doorway to Hell. Orpheus is somewhere in one of these chilly pits from which voices ring forth. Suddenly, at the very end of the maze, in a blaze of light, someone stepped onto an enormous limestone pedestal, a slender person in a vast hooded white cloak: Jean Cocteau. So he ap-

[1] Jean Cocteau's junior assistant for *Testament of Orpheus.* Today he is a film critic and producer of film shorts.

peared to us for the first time, true to his legend: the two little proba-
tioners with their heads full of his books and tales of his glory, see the
real man.

There was the world of the poet and the great; and another, very
tiny, of the subordinate couple, working in the anthill.

From time to time, between two plane trips, someone paid attention
to us. Several people were surprised not to see us at lunch when everyone
ate together at the restaurant; and Cocteau, kindly, offered us a book
inscribed by him. All around him swirled a court, soliciting his advice,
disappearing, swelling again.

And he, perpetually playing a role, welcomes, counsels, darts off. To
two young people, come to shoot the film of films with their 16 mm.
camera he says: "I like poetry which creates itself. . . . I bequeath it to
the young who have been of great assistance to me . . . a young generation
starved for something truer than the truth, who do not want to see again
on the screen what they see everyday at home. . . . There is also a second
youth which is not recognized; it takes a long time to discover it." He
closes into himself, paces, his two index fingers pressed to his temples;
for a moment he watches me work on the preparation of a shot, then
wheels around and tosses out: "I don't know what's the matter with them,
but most of the young people today are not very lively."

He is ill at ease; he cannot stand to remain inactive for a second;
he returns to his own dreamy gypsies, men of the world, men-horses. He
hums, beating out a rhythm with his fingertips on the corner of a prop.
He comes and goes; speaks first with one, then with another; he squints
through the eyepiece of the camera; he sits, stands, jokes. . . .

And we don't understand; we don't dare learn to separate the true
from the false.

Cocteau knows his own face, and it frightens him. One evening after
seeing the rushes, he furiously attacked the cameraman: "You see that!
One might say an old monkey . . . I look like a cheese. . . . I know that
I'm an old man, but even so! And my nose . . . my nose!" That evening
he was wearing his Oxford suit on the screen and we thought we were
seeing a disappointed socialite, petty and egotistical, who was angry at

himself for being old. But abruptly his transparent eyes become animated, and he is transformed; his eyes catch ours fixed upon him, and seek contact. But we flee his glance in turn: we feel awkward and are afraid of being humiliated.

There are times when we detest him, along with the artificial world that ceaselessly builds around him. At the same time we are fascinated by his toughness when he takes refuge in the work of an actor and then, after a take, becomes his own most ferocious critic, imagining the trembling of his hand, the stiffness of an expression, or fearing a loss of humor. He tenaciously endures delays and waiting: "They don't want me to make this film. But who are they'? I don't know. Day before yesterday, Tiresias; yesterday, the children, today, the car! . . . But I will have this film! I'll make it, and no one will stop me from making it!"

Little by little, we too learn disrespect. Then we understand that Cocteau crosses over the shooting as a tightrope walker crosses above the crowd over which he hangs on his steel wire, anxious for the result and ignoring the rest, the spitefulness of rebellious things: the jamming cameras, the weakening troupe, the hungry crew. "But what's happening . . . what's happening?" says he, sorrowfully, at such moments.

"We must take into account the insoluble. . . . What Doudou[1] will have to do is quite difficult, so, I would like the camera stationary, no tamping or anything like that. . . . Unfortunately, it's a reversal, and in slow motion!"

And, at the projection, he marvels that something as closed and hostile as the camera produces such beautiful things. To Pinoteau: "Who would have guessed, Claude, who would have guessed that this collection of sheets would be so beautiful? . . . The cinema is always astounding." He continually proclaims that irreality has its own strict rules; he bows to them, and we begin to discover in him a form of magic thought that enables him to integrate the disorder of coincidences into a vast conspiracy of order. They shoot the death of the poet. The javelin thrown by Minerva pierces him and protrudes from his breast. He brings his hands up to the wound, falls to his knees, collapses murmuring: "How awful . . . how

[1] Nickname for Edouard Dermit. Dermit became Cocteau's adopted son.—ED.

awful!" At the same instant, the sound of a jet airplane splits the quarries. Everyone panics; he is delighted.

What interests him above everything else is the part played by chance. In editing, he will always choose a take as a function of whatever it presents of an unexpected nature; while running the moviola backward, he will often find himself regretting that he had not filmed a shot in slow motion or in reverse. He wants phenomena to link themselves up gratuitously, for people and objects to acquire a strangeness that defies analysis; he seeks the inexplicable breach in the order of things through which the marvelous will enter to attack that order.

In fact, he paints, writes dialogues, adds scenes, always seeking—finally finds the idea of the tribunal with the Princess and Heurtebise. It is the quest for a responsibility, the accusation of the poet, "a good sound thrashing."

During the shooting of the scene at Saint-Maurice, a silence lengthens, a word; contact catches, still feeble. One evening, after a very hard day, he waited a long time with Doudou while I finished cleaning up in order to drive me home. We stop at rue Montpensier. He is drained by fatigue. He speaks to me at great length about the genius of Buñuel, Genêt, and Picasso. I remember his timidity, his fear of Picasso during the shooting. Henceforth, a real dialogue settles in.

Later, despite appearances, I began to recognize a tragic man; over and over I recall his meeting with Oedipus on the rough path, and hear his voice: "Whatever one has wished too ardently to meet, will someday pass by without being seen."

ANDRÉ FRAIGNEAU

A Fabulous Opera

Slow minds, like Gide, accused him of "skipping steps." He climbs them more quickly than the others: there's the truth. The proof is that, his exploit accomplished, he turns around and patiently, precisely points out each step to be taken if one is to rejoin him . . . which he is burning for us to do, since solitude horrifies him. Of course, once we catch up with him there is no respite from the disputation of his title to pioneer and maverick, to which he has the right. This misadventure has happened so often and is, one might say, "so human," that one is astonished to see that it surprises Cocteau, and causes him to suffer as if it were the first time. But a period of "What good is it all?" of variable duration, in which the poet declares that he will never do anything again, is succeeded by a new venture into which he enters wholeheartedly.

I have spoken of Cocteau, "professor of energy." Everyone who has seen him work or has worked with him speaks of him with slightly frightened astonishment. And who has ever seen him other than at work? When he is preparing a theatrical, cinematographical, or graphic work, Cocteau becomes the entire organism of which he ought to represent only the head. His passion for craftsmanship, his quick-wittedness, and his skill with his hands enable him to assimilate a wide range of techniques. He speaks to each specialist as a professional, and could have replaced any of them at a moment's notice, from the chief actor to the assistant electrician. Day and night he assumes all responsibilities. One is reminded of Rimbaud's phrase: "I became a fabulous opera."

His persuasive force is so great that I have seen the technicians working with him on theatre stages, in radio and cinema studios, begin to speak, gesticulate, and become excited after his fashion. This involuntary and often comic mimicry certainly testifies to the grip of his personality, but that's not the important thing. Other animating spirits know how to make themselves popular. Cocteau never made concessions or changed his style in order to please. Briand would have said of him what he said of the orator Barrès, "He has no loose change." But his gold pieces are in circulation. To fill the neighborhood theatres with a film like *Orpheus* gives the lie to those imperatives that insist on rating public taste at an ignoble level. The public is sensitive to grandeur when it is presented to them with unquestionable faith and authority. Further, the public recognizes and loves a job well done.

(*Cocteau par lui-même,* Editions du Seuil)

Testament of Orpheus: **Jean Marais and Jean Cocteau.**

JEAN MARAIS

At the Peak of One's Pitch

Never did Jean Cocteau give me an intonation. Never did he seek to straighten a crooked rail or curve a straight one! Never did he advise a gesture.

His method is different: to live, speak, look at beautiful things together, to cultivate the soul without thinking of art—which in his eyes is no more than a margin of life.

With him, group effort is not a dream of cinematographic journalism.

I can verify that he never selected even a mechanic without taking into account the temperament of the entire crew; there is no such thing as either first or last place; from top to bottom everyone must regard himself as a friend of the enterprise and consecrate himself to it with all his heart.

The result is an atmosphere of willingness and helpfulness that banishes fatigue and that Cocteau believes the special-effects camera captures.

I don't believe that he prefers one form of art to another; I believe he throws himself headfirst, and without the slightest caution, into the mine he proposes to explore.

He believes that one doesn't know the public, and knows even less what it wants, and that the only way to touch men's souls is to express oneself at peak pitch and to dare to encounter souls attuned to our wavelength.

It is only in reading Jean Cocteau, living in his house, breathing the calm and beneficent air that he breathes, that one is able to learn from him the marvelous things he personifies; he hates schools, trials and auditions; he radiates a strength my pen cannot render, but of which my friendship and admiration are intensely aware.

(Empreintes, Brussels, 1950)

ANDRÉ MAUROIS

Your Mysteries Remain Opaque

. . . . The art of the screen tempted you. You have succeeded in it, and it is one of the domains to which your contribution has been incomparable. You were one of the first writers to comprehend that cinematography, in addition to fiction and the theatre, can engender works of art. The film-maker writes "with an ink of light," but the laws of style are the same for him as for all artists: a rigorous simplicity, a rhythm, a modest obedience to professional necessities. Although the camera and rail make the pace drag, each has its special properties that the great artist calls into play, just as Michelangelo drew his rarest beauties from defects in the marble.

. . . . *The Blood of a Poet, Beauty and the Beast, The Eternal Return, Orpheus,* are, and will remain, classics in every country of the world. Like the great English humorists, you have understood that the stranger a tale, the more important it is that the teller be realistic. . . . Swift imposes a rigorous precision when he describes the extravagant worlds through which he leads Gulliver. You surround death with motorcyclists similar to those used by the prefecture of police; you replace the tribunal of hell with bureaucrats in normal attire; you receive coded messages by wireless from the great beyond. . . . You remember this quip from an eighteenth-century man to whom a woman said: "I love you because . . ." "Ah! madame," said he, "if you know why, then I am lost!" To a commentator who would translate your *Orpheus* into clear languages, I am convinced you would reply: "Ah! Sir, if you understand what I wanted to say, then it is because I have said it badly." Be reassured, sir, your mysteries remain opaque, and you are safe. We leave your films with the confused feeling that the singular worlds you have created possess, like all this vast universe, a sublime and hidden sense. You love the supernatural, but you know that nature is supernatural and itself the permanent miracle. You are a prodigious animator and you have shaped your epoch through the most diverse art forms. The poet Coleridge said: "I don't believe in phantoms; I've seen too many of them." You would have the right to say: "I don't follow modes; I've set too many of them." One can no longer count the number of writers, painters, musicians, filmmakers, and actors who owe their renown to you and who deserve it. Your choices of yesterday are today, all over the world, the classics of everyone.

> (Reply to Jean Cocteau's discourse,
> upon his admission to the Académie
> française, 1955. Editions Gallimard)

ROGER PILLAUDIN

Pages from the Journal of Jean Cocteau's Film

Monday, 7 September 1959

They photograph him photographing.

Pontoiseau,[1] in his sphinxlike language, finishes the final details of his illumination.

"Tighten up the 5 on the wall a little bit. Tap it lightly. Stop! Tighten

---

[1] Director of photography for *Testament.*—ED.

a little. . . . Go on, a little more! Pull up a little. No, tap! Turn the 500
to the left. Hold! A shutter on the left. That's fine, thanks. . . ."

A last glance in his viewfinder. Satisfied, he relights his pipe.

The chief electrician, to calm everyone, extinguishes all the lights.

Everything is plunged in gloom.

Then, a cry:

"—Lights!"

With a single stroke, the walls blaze.

In the center of the stage, resplendent, as though sprung from the
night (he arrived there, groping): Jean Cocteau.

Did the stage crew do it on purpose? The apparition was fantastic, as if
to illustrate the first line of *Testament of Orpheus*:

"His name was Jean, he was not of the darkness, but he appeared to
make witness to the darkness." [1]

Cocteau was wearing light-gray slacks, a yellow leather jacket, a pale
mauve shirt, a black tie, light shoes. On his ringfinger, the famous six-
hooped ring.

Cocteau sticks his eye to the lense, checks the focus, modifies the set
slightly, explains to Pinoteau the way he intends to play the scene, and
steps into position, tossing out a joyous:

"Let's go, les enfants!"

Cocteau turns his back to the camera. Facing him, standing behind his
table, is the baldheaded bailiff: Brynner.

PINOTEAU: *Roll 'em!*

Clapper: Testament 209, #1.

The poet is now before the seventh door, and Jean Cocteau acts for the
first time.

BAILIFF: *Here, abandon all hope.* (He bows.)

The Poet, back glued to the camera, moves toward him, hiding Brynner's
bowed form. Before the table he bows. The bailiff straightens.

POET: *I thought so. Must I sign my name anyway?*

The Poet exits, passing the bailiff, who eyes him up and down, moves
away to the back of the set, turns and regards the bailiff fearfully.

[1] Cut out in editing.

PINOTEAU: *Cut. Okay for you, Raichi?*

RAICHI: *I can see Mr. Brynner when Mr. Cocteau moves toward him.*

COCTEAU: *Ah! That won't do. He mustn't be seen. . . . Only when I bow before him.*

PINOTEAU: *Okay, we'll do a retake.*

They start again.

RAICHI: *I can still see him. Mr. Cocteau should hold his arms out from his sides slightly to make his body bigger.*

Retake.

The bailiff can still be seen. Cocteau deviated slightly from the axis of the lens.

COCTEAU: *Draw a line on the ground. I'll follow it.*

PINOTEAU: *Ready! This is the good one.*

BRYNNER: *Please say "Action" to me. If not, I don't know when to begin.*

PINOTEAU: *Will you say it, Jean?*

COCTEAU: *No. When I'm on camera, you take over the orders. Yul, I'd like you to repeat your line twice: "Here . . . (pause), abandon all hope."*

BRYNNER: *Yes, okay.*

Retake.

PINOTEAU: *Cut. It's good. Should we dub it?*

It is dubbed. Notes. Photographs.

Behind Cocteau, always attentive, affectionate, the frail Mme. Weisweiller. She urges him to sit, rest, cover himself up. But he is always on his feet, surveying everything, continually on the move, and refuses his shawl.

(Editions de la Table Ronde)

FILMOGRAPHY

The "Major Filmography" is made up of those films written and directed by Jean Cocteau. "Filmography II" consists of those films for which he wrote either the scenario or the dialogue, and on which he had a marked influence. This study has dealt with the works in these two categories. "Filmography III" gathers together either those films in which Cocteau's collaboration was minor, films about him or about his graphic works, and films based on one or another of his literary works.

MAJOR FILMOGRAPHY

1930: *Le Sang d'un poète* (*The Blood of a Poet*)

Production, editing, commentary: JEAN COCTEAU. Technical assistants: Michel J. Arnaud and Louis Page. Special Effects: Georges Périnal. Assistant: Preben Engberg. Sound: Henri Labrély, R.C.A. Photophone. Sets: J. G. d'Eaubonne. Stage Photographer: Sacha Mansour. Music: Georges Auric. Orchestre Flament. Actors: Lee Miller (THE STATUE), Enrique Rivero (THE POET), Pauline Carton (CHILD'S TUTOR), Féral Benga (BLACK ANGEL), Jean Desbordes (THE CHARACTER OF LOUIS XV, MASKED), Odette Talazac, Barbette, Fernand Dichamp, Lucien Jager (AUDIENCE).

The film was produced April–September, 1930. Public premiere at the Théâtre du Vieux-Colombier, Paris, January 20, 1932. Released in the United States on November 13, 1933, under the title *Le Sang d'un poète*. United States distributor: Brandon Films.

1945: *La Belle et la Bête* (*Beauty and the Beast*)

Scenario, dialogue, direction: JEAN COCTEAU. Technical Adviser: René Clément. Director of Photography: Henri Alekan. Cameraman: Tiquet. Costumes: Christian Bérard. Sets: Christian Bérard, executed by René Moulaert. Editing: Claude Ibéria. Music: Georges Auric. Sound: J. Lebreton. Actors: Jean Marais (AVENANT, THE BEAST, THE PRINCE), Josette Day

(BEAUTY), Mila Parély, Nane Germon (BEAUTY'S SISTER), Marcel André (BEAUTY'S FATHER), Michel Auclair (LUDOVIC, BEAUTY'S BROTHER). Producer: André Paulvé. Production Director: E. Darbon. Distribution: Discina.

Paris premiere: January, 1946. Released in the United States on January 15, 1948, under the title *Beauty and the Beast*. United States distributor: Lopert.

1947: *L'Aigle à deux têtes* (*The Eagle with Two Heads*)

Scenario, dialogue, direction: JEAN COCTEAU. Technical Assistant: H. Bromberger. Director of Photography: Christian Matras. Cameraman: Alain Douarinou. Editing: Claude Ibéria. Artistic direction (models, sets, and costumes): Christian Bérard, executed by Wakhéwitch and Morin (sets) and Escoffier (costumes), Zay, Bataille. Music: Georges Auric. Sound: Longuet. Actors: Edwige Feuillère (THE QUEEN), Jean Marais (STANISLAS), Sylvia Monfort (EDITH DE BERG), Jean Debucourt (POLICE CHIEF), Jacques Varennes, Gilles Quéant, Abdallah, M. Mazyl, E. Stirling, Yvonne de Bray. Producer: Ariane Films-Sirius.

Shot primarily at the Château de Vizille, in October, 1947.

Paris premiere, September, 1947.

Released in the United States on December 15, 1948, under the title *The Eagle with Two Heads*.

1948: *Les Parents terribles*

Scenario, dialogues: text from the play by JEAN COCTEAU. Direction: JEAN COCTEAU. Director of Photography: Michel Kelber. Cameraman: Tiquet. Sets: Guy de Gastyne, under the artistic direction of Christian Bérard. Music: Georges Auric. Sound: Archimbault. Editor: Jacqueline Sadoul. Actors: Jean Marais (MICHEL), Yvonne de Bray (YVONNE-SOPHIE), Gabrielle Dorziat (LÉO), Marcel André (GEORGES), Josette Day (MADELEINE). Producer: Ariane: Alexandre Mnouchkine and Francis Cosne.

Filmed from May to June, 1948, in the Studio Francœur. Paris premiere: November, 1948.

Distribution: Sirius. Released in the United States in 1954 under the title *Intimate Relations*. United States distributor: Brandon Films.

1950: *Orphée (Orpheus)*
Scenario, dialogue, direction: JEAN COCTEAU. Director of Photography: Nicolas Hayer. Sets: d'Eaubonne. Costumes: Escoffier (Bérard, just before his death, had begun to design the models for the sets and the sketches for the costumes). Sound: J. Calvet. Music: Georges Auric. Actors: Jean Marais (ORPHEUS), Maria Casarès (THE PRINCESS), Marie Déa (EURYDICE), François Périer (HEURTEBISE), Henri Crémieux, R. Blin, Juliette Gréco (AGLAONICE), Edouard Dermit (CÉGESTE), Pierre Bertin, Jacques Varennes. Producer: André Paulvé and Films du Palais-Royal.

Filmed in the fall of 1949. First showing: Film Week, Cannes, March 1, 1950. Paris premiere, the end of September, 1950.

International Critics' Prize, Venice, 1950.

Distribution: Discina International. Released in the United States on November 22, 1950, under the title *Orpheus*.

1950: *Coriolan*
16 mm. film; filmed for fun during two weekends in the country with Jean Marais and Josette Day.

1952: *La Villa Santo-Sospir*
Filmed in 16 mm. Kodachrome; produced and improvised by Jean Cocteau in the villa of Mme. Alec Weisweiller at Saint-Jean-Cap-Ferrat. Cocteau often spent time there, and had decorated the walls. In this film he shoots his own designs, the grounds, the garden, and himself.

Neither this film nor *Coriolan* has ever been distributed commercially.

1960: *Le Testament d'Orphée (Testament of Orpheus)*
Scenario, dialogue, direction: JEAN COCTEAU. Technical collaborator: Claude Pinoteau. Director of Photography: R. Pontoiseau. Cameraman: Raichi. Sound: Bertrand. Editing: Marie-Josèphe Yoyotte. Actors: Jean Cocteau (THE POET), Edouard Dermit (CÉGESTE), Henri Crémieux (THE SCIENTIST), Jean-Pierre Léaud, Alice Saprich, Françoise Christophe. With the friendly collaboration of: Yul Brynner (BAILIFF), Daniel Gélin, Maria

Casarès, François Périer repeating their roles from *Orpheus;* Charles Aznavour, Picasso, L.-M. Dominguin, Lucia Bosé, Jean Marais (*Oedipus*), Serge Lifar, Henry Torrès (who questions the little girl during the radio interview). Producer: Jean Thuillier, les Editions Cinégraphiques.

Filmed at Les Baux, Studios de la Victorine, Nice, from September to October, 1959. Paris premiere: 1960.

Distribution: Cinédis. Released in the United States on April 9, 1962, under the title *Testament of Orpheus.* United States distributor: Brandon Films.

FILMOGRAPHY II

1943: *Le Baron fantôme* (*The Phantom Baron*)

Scenario: Serge de Poligny. Adaptation: Poligny, Louis Chavance. Dialogue: JEAN COCTEAU. Direction: Serge de Poligny. Director of Photography: Roger Hubert. Sets: Krauss. Music: Louis Beydts. Actors: Odette Joyeux, Jany Holt, A. Lefaur, Alain Cuny, A. Clariond, Claude Sainval, Marguerite Pierry.

Filmed in September, 1942. Paris premiere, June, 1943.

1943: *L'Eternal Retour* (*The Eternal Return*)

Scenario, dialogue: JEAN COCTEAU. Direction: Jean Delannoy. Director of photography: Roger Hubert. Sets: Wakhévitch. Music: Georges Auric. Actors: Jean Marais (PATRICE), Madeleine Sologne (NATHALIE), Jean Murat (MARC), Piéral (ACHILLE), Alexandre Rignault (LE MORHOLT), Junie Astor (NATHALIE II), Roland Toutain (LIONEL), Jeanne Marken (MARIE-ANNE), Jean d'Yd, Yvonne de Bray (GERTRUDE), Producer: André Paulvé. Production director: Emile Darbon.

Filmed in March, 1943, La Victorine, Nice. Paris premiere, October, 1943.

Distribution: Discina.

1947: *Ruy Blas*

Scenario, dialogue: JEAN COCTEAU. Direction: Pierre Billon. Assistant: M. Boisrond. Director of Photography: Michel Kelber. Cameraman: Louis

Stein. Sets: Georges Wakhéwitch. Music: Georges Auric. Actors: Jean Marais (RUY BLAS, ZAFARI), Danielle Darrieux (THE QUEEN), Gabrielle Dorziat (THE DUCHESS OF ALBUQUERQUE), Marcel Herrand (DON SALLUSTE), Alexandre Rignault, Paul Amiot, Gilles Quéant, Ionne Salinas, Jovanni Grasso, Charles Lemontier, Lurville, J. Berlioz, P. Magnier. Producer: André Paulvé.

Filmed in the summer of 1947. Paris premiere, February, 1948.

1950: *Les Enfants terribles*
Adaptation and dialogue: JEAN COCTEAU. Direction: J.-P. Melville. Director of Photography: Henri Decaë. Sets: Mathys. Actors: Nicole Stéphane (ELISABETH), Edouard Dermit (PAUL), Renée Cosima (DARGELOS and AGATHE), Jacques Bernard, Mel Martin, Roger Gaillard. Producer: J.-P. Melville. Distribution: Gaumont.

FILMOGRAPHY III

1942: *Comédie du bonheur*
Adaptation and dialogue: JEAN COCTEAU, from the play by Nicolas Evreïnof. Direction: Marcel l'Herbier. Sets: René Moulaert. Music: Jacques Ibert. Actors: Michel Simon, Ramon Novarro, Jacqueline Delubac, Micheline Presle, Sylvie, Alerme, Louis Jourdan. Director of Production: G. Lampin.

Filmed in Rome. Paris premiere, July, 1946.

1945: *Les Dames du Bois de Boulogne*
Dialogue: JEAN COCTEAU. Adaptation and Direction: Robert Bresson (from an episode in *Jacques le Fataliste* by Diderot). Director of Photography: Ph. Agostini. Sets: Max Douy. Music: Jean-Jacques Gruenwald. Actors: Paul Bernard, Maria Casarès, Elina Labourdette, Lucienne Bogaert.

1947: *La Voix humaine*
Film by Roberto Rossellini, from a play by JEAN COCTEAU. Sets: Christian Bérard. Actress: Anna Magnani.

1948: *La Legend de Sainte Ursule*
An art film by Luciano Emmer after the Vittore Carpaccio painting in Venice. Commentary by JEAN COCTEAU.

1948: *Les Noces de sable*
Film by André Zvoboda (adapted from a Moroccan legend similar to Tristan and Yseult). Commentary written and spoken by JEAN COCTEAU.

1951: *Le Rossignol de l'Empereur de Chine*
Marionette film by Jiri Trnka. French commentary written and spoken by JEAN COCTEAU.

1951: *Venise et ses amants*
Commentary, film by Emmer and Gras.

1952: *La Corona negra* (*La Couronne noire* or *The Black Crown*)
Franco-Spanish film by Luis Saslavsky, based on a scenario by JEAN COCTEAU. Dialogue: Miguel Mihura. Spanish collaborators. Actors: María Félix, V. Gassmann, Rossano Brazzi, Piéral.

1952: Prefatory text to *La Porte de l'Enfer* by Kinugasa

1953: Commentary for *Le Rouge est mis* by I. Barrère and H. Knapp

1954: *Une Melodie, cinq peintres*
A German short by Hergert Seggelke. JEAN COCTEAU is one of the painters. He draws behind and on a window.

1957: *A l'Aube de monde*
Film short by René Lucot. Commentary by JEAN COCTEAU.

1957: *Le Bel indifférent*
Film short by Jacques Demy, adapted from the one-act play of the same

title by JEAN COCTEAU. Sets: B. Evein. Music: M. Jarre. Actors: Jeanne Allard, Angelo Bellini.

1958: *Le Musée Grévin*
   Film by Jean Masson, directed by Jacques Demy. One Cocteau sequence: JEAN COCTEAU improvises and acts out a dialogue scene with his double in the Musée Grévin.

1958: Prefatory text of P. Paviot's film short *Django Reinhardt*

1959: *Saint-Blaise-des Simples*
   Scenario and commentary: Jean-Jacques Kihm. Producer: Philippe Joulia. Director of Photography: Pierre Fattori. Music: Francine Tremblot. Production: Les Films Septentrion.
   Filmed in the old chapel of the Leper Hospital at Milly-la-Forêt that JEAN COCTEAU had decorated.

1961: Adaptation of *La Princesse de Clèves* for Jean Delannoy.

BIBLIOGRAPHY

French and English

Jean Cocteau's literary, dramatic, and cinematographic work is so intertwined that a bibliography dealing only with works directly related to film would have been too limited. Thus we have included literary and dramatic works, and works of general criticism by and about Cocteau. For reasons of space, however, our bibliography is limited. See Elizabeth Sprigge and Jean-Jacques Kihm's *Jean Cocteau: The Man and the Mirror* for a complete bibliography.

WORKS BY JEAN COCTEAU

I. Screenplays, Film Dialogues

L'Aigle à deux têtes. Screenplay and dialogue. Collection "Lo Duca."

La Belle et la Bête: Album. Editions du Pré-aux-Clercs.

    Beauty and the Beast (appears in *Three Screenplays,* Orion Press/Grossman, 1968).

Les Dames du Bois de Boulogne. Dialogue published in *Les Cahiers du Cinéma,* Nos. 75–77, October, November, and December, 1957.

L'Eternel Retour. Nouvelles Editions françaises, 1948.

La Légende de Sainte-Ursule. Commentary for Luciano Emmer's film. Published in *Poésie critique* (Editions Gallimard).

Orphée. Editions André Bonne, 1951.

Les Parents terribles. Screenplay published by *Le Monde Illustré,* No. 37, December 11, 1948.

Ruy Blas. Text of the film adaptation. Morihien, 1947.

Le Sang d'un Poète (with photographs by Sacha Mansour). Editions du Rocher, 1948. With drawings by Jean Cocteau. Editions du Rocher, 1957.

    The Blood of a Poet; a film. Translated by Lily Pons. Bodley Press, New York, 1949.

    The Blood of a Poet (appears in *Three Screenplays,* Orion Press/Grossman, 1968).

Le Testament d'Orphée. Screenplay. Photographs by Lucien Clergue. Editions du Rocher, 1960.

    The Testament of Orpheus (appears in *Three Screenplays,* Orion Press/Grossman, 1968).

Three Screenplays and Other Writings on the Cinema (*The Blood of a Poet, Beauty and the Beast, The Testament of Orpheus*). Orion Press/Grossman, New York, 1968.

II. Plays

L'Aigle à deux têtes. Gallimard, 1946.

    The Eagle with Two Heads (appears in *Five Plays,* Hill & Wang, 1961).

    The Eagle Has Two Heads. Adapted by Ronald Duncan. Vision Press, London, 1948.

Orphée. Stock, Paris, 1927.

    *Orpheus (*appears in *The Infernal Machine: and Other Plays,* New Directions, 1963).

Orphée (appears in *Five Plays,* Hill & Wang, 1961).

Orphée: A Tragedy in One Act and an Interval. Translated by Carl Wildman. Oxford University Press, London, 1933.

Les Parents terribles. Gallimard, Paris, 1938.

Intimate Relations (appears in *Five Plays,* Hill & Wang, 1961).

La Voix humaine. Stock, Paris, 1930.

The Human Voice. Translated by Carl Wildman. Vision, London, 1951.

Five Plays, Hill & Wang, New York, 1961. *Orphée, Antigone* (adapted from Sophocles), *Intimate Relations (Les Parents terribles), The Holy Terrors (Les Monstres sacrés), The Eagle with Two Heads (L'Aigle à deux têtes).*

The Infernal Machine: And Other Plays. New Directions, New York, 1963. *The Infernal Machine (La Machine infernale), Orpheus (Orphée), The Eiffel Tower Wedding Party (Les Mariés de la Tour Eiffel), The Knights of the Round Table (Chevaliers de la Table Ronde), Bacchus, The Speaker's Text of Oedipus Rex.*

III. Novels

Les Enfants terribles. B. Grasset, Paris, 1929.

The Children of the Game. Translated by Rosamond Lehmann. New Directions, New York, 1956.

Enfants terribles. Translated by Samuel Putnam. Brewer & Warren, Inc., New York, 1930.

Le Grand Ecart. Librairie Stock, Paris, 1924.

The Big Mistake. Translated by Dorothy Williams. P. Owen, London, 1958 (also called *The Miscreant*).

The Grand Ecart. Translated by Lewis Galantière. G. P. Putnam, New York and London, 1925.

Thomas l'imposteur. Nouvelle Revue française, Paris, 1923.

The Impostor. Translated by Dorothy Williams. P. Owen, London, 1947.

Thomas the Impostor. Translated by Lewis Galantière. D. Appleton & Co., New York, 1925.

IV. Works by or Interviews with Cocteau Concerned Primarily with Film

La Belle et la Bête, Journal d'un film. J.-B. Janin, Paris, 1946. Republished by Editions du Rocher, Monaco, 1958.

Diary of a Film (La Belle et la Bête). Translated by Ronald Duncan. D. Dobson, London, 1950.

Cinéma, un œil ouvert sur le monde. Ed. by G.-M. Bovay (book collaborated on by Cocteau and others). Editions Clairefontaine, Lausanne, 1952.

Entretiens autour du cinématographe. Gathered by André Fraigneau. Editions André Bonne, Paris, 1951.

    Cocteau on the Film. A conversation recorded by André Fraigneau. Translated by Vera Traill. Roy Publishers, New York, 1954.

Jean Marais. Calmann-Lévy. (Collection "Masques et Visages"). Paris, 1951.

Journal du Testament d'Orphée (Roger Pillaudin). Editions de la Table Ronde, Paris, 1960.

On the Film. Dufour, Chester Springs, Pa., 1954.

Orson Welles (by Cocteau and André Bazin). Chavane, Paris, 1950.

V. General Works (in English)

The Difficulty of Being. Introduction by Ned Rorem. Translated from *La difficulté d'être* (1947) by Elizabeth Sprigge. Coward-McCann, New York, 1967.

The Hand of a Stranger. Authorized translation by Alec Brown of *Journal d'un inconnu*. Elek Books, London, 1956.

The Journals of Jean Cocteau. Edited and translated with an introduction by Wallace Fowlie. Indiana University Press, Bloomington, 1964.

My Contemporaries. Edited and introduced by Margaret Crosland. Owen, London, 1967.

WORKS ABOUT JEAN COCTEAU

I. General Critical Studies

Margaret Crosland. *Jean Cocteau: A Biography,* Knopf, New York, 1956.

Pierre Dubourg. *Dramaturgie de Jean Cocteau*. Foreword by Thierry Maulnier. Grasset, Paris, 1954.

Wallace Fowlie. *Jean Cocteau: The History of a Poet's Age*. Indiana University Press, Bloomington, 1966.

André Fraigneau. *Cocteau*. Translated by Donald Lehmkuhl (Evergreen

Profile Books). Grove Press, New York, 1961.

André Fraigneau. *Jean Cocteau par lui-même.* Editions du Seuil, Paris, 1957.

Jean-Jacques Kihm. *Cocteau.* Gallimard, Paris, 1960.

Roger Lannes. *Jean Cocteau.* Essay followed by a group of poems selected by Henri Parisot. Editions Seghers (Collection "Poètes d'Aujourd'hui").

Claude Mauriac. *Jean Cocteau ou la verité du mensonge.* O. Lieutier, Paris, 1945.

Neal Oxenhandler. *Scandal and Parade: The Theater of Jean Cocteau.* Rutgers University Press, New Brunswick, N. J., 1957.

Karl Günter Simon. *Jean Cocteau oder Die Poesie in Film.* Rembrandt Verlag, Berlin, Zehlendorf, 1958.

Elizabeth Sprigge and Jean-Jacques Kihm. *Jean Cocteau: The Man and the Mirror.* Coward-McCann, New York, 1968.

II. Articles in English on Cocteau as a Filmmaker

John Peale Bishop. "A Film of Jean Cocteau [Blood of a Poet]." *The Collected Essays of John Peale Bishop.* Scribner, New York, 1948.

Maria Casarès. "On Cocteau as a Film Director." *World Theatre,* Vol. 8, No. 1, p. 51; Spring, 1959.

Francis Koval. "Interview with Cocteau." *Sight and Sound,* 1950.

Neal Oxenhandler. "On Cocteau." *Film Quarterly,* Fall, 1964.

C. G. Wallis. "The Blood of a Poet." *Kenyon Review,* Vol. 6, No. 1, pp. 24–42; Winter, 1944.

III. Miscellaneous

Journals: Special Issues:
   Empreintes (testimonials, photocopies of letters and handwritten texts). Editions L'Ecran du Monde. Brussels, May, 1950.
   La Table Ronde, No. 94, October, 1955.

For studies devoted exclusively to Cocteau's cinematographic works, refer particularly to *Cahiers du cinéma, Cinéma 55* and following issues, to *Télé-Ciné, L'Ecran français,* and also to the chapters dealing with Cocteau in the following works:

Henri Agel. *Les Grands Cinéastes*. Editions Universitaires.

André Bazin. *What Is Cinema?* University of California, 1967 (translation of *Qu'est-ce que le cinéma?* Editions du Cerf, Paris, 1958–62).

Claude Mauriac. *Petite Littérature du cinéma*. Editions du Cerf, Paris.

George Sadoul. *Le Cinéma français*. Editions Flammarion, Paris, 1962.

DISCOGRAPHY

A selection of French and English recordings relevant to Cocteau's cinematographic work:

Le Bel indifférent. Edith Piaf. (La Voix de son Maître, FS. 1021, 33 t., 25 cm).

The Infernal Machine (La Machine infernale). Margaret Leighton, Diane Cilento. Translated by Carl Wildman. Caedmon TRS 321 (1968).

Jean Cocteau: A Self-Portrait. Conversation in French with William Fifield on June 9, 1962. Caedmon TC 1199.

La Voix humaine. Gaby Morlay (Decca FMT 163622, 33 t., 30 cm); Berthe Bovy (Pathé, DTX 288, 33 t., illustrated jacket album); Simone Signoret (Polydor).

The Human Voice. Ingrid Bergman. Translated by Maximilian Ilyin, directed by Howard Sackler. Caedmon TC 1118 (1961).

PHONOGRAPHY

A selection of recordings held by the central record library of Radiodiffusion-Télévision française.[1]

Interviews and Talks by Jean Cocteau:

Talk on Radiguet, December 15, 1943, 15 minutes. Evocation of *La Voix humaine* by Berthe Bovy, January 29, 1947. Interview on *L'Aigle à deux*

---

[1] Use of this material requires permission from the Direction des Services Artistiques of Radiodiffusion-Télévision française. For further information write to the New York office of the R.T.F., 1290 Avenue of the Americas.

têtes, September 21, 1948, in *Demain au Cinéma.* Homage to Christian Bérard, February 20, 1949. Presentation of *Les Noces de sable,* May 15, 1949. On Orson Welles, in *Les Rois de la nuit,* November 27, 1949. Interview on *Orphée* and *Les Enfants terribles,* December 31, 1949. Program "Incompatabilité d'humeur," interview with Cocteau, Jean Négroni called *Cocardes,* the poem on cinema. Testimonial to Christian Bérard, program "L'Art et la vie," February 23, 1950. Conversations between Cocteau and Fraigneau, January 26–March 28, 1951. The eighth interview (*Le Sang d'un poète*). The thirteenth interview (*La Belle et la Bête, Les Parents terribles*). On the Cannes Film Festival, over which he was presiding, March 26 and March 31, 1954.

Poetry, art according to Cocteau, in *Pleins feux sur les spectacles du monde,* October 7, 1955. Interview with Cocteau on *Tels qu'en eux-mêmes,* 15 minutes. Discourse to the Académie française, October 20, 1955. Discourse to the Académie royale of Belgium, October 25, 1955. Conference given at the French Pavilion of the World's Fair in Brussels: "Les Armes secrètes de la France," September 20, 1958. Interview on Jean Desbordes, August 3, 1959.
Le Testament d'Orphée, program by Roger Pillaudin, September, 1959.

Selection of R.T.F. recordings of works by Jean Cocteau that have been adapted for the cinema:
La Voix humaine, Gaby Morlay, July 27, 1944; Berthe Bovy, May 25, 1947; Louise Conte, June 9, 1954.
Le Bel indifférent, Yvonne de Bray, November 24, 1949.
Les Parents terribles, Yvonne de Bray, G. Dorziat, M. André, J. Day, Jean Marais, February 10, 1954.
Orphée, J.-P. Aumont, Monique Mélinand, Michel Bouquet, Maria Casarès, Jean Topart, Sacha Pitoëff, June 9, 1954.
L'Aigle à deux têtes, E. Feuillère, Jean Marais. (1) Sylvia Monfort, Jacques Varennes, August 22, 1954. (2) Suzy Prim, Claude Génia, Julien Bertheau, André Falcon, Jacques Varennes, January 16, 1956.

Adaptation of *Les Enfants terribles*. Adaptation by Agathe Mella. Music by Henri Sauguet. Jean Marais, J. Day, Jean Cocteau, Sylvia Monfort, March 14, 1947.

Adaptation of *L'Eternel Retour,* story and dialogue by Jean Cocteau, Adaptation for radio by G. Beaume, music by Georges Auric, with Jean Marais, Michèle Alfa, Yvonne de Bray, J. Marchat, R. Larquey, Piéral, Louise Conte, Daniel Ivernel, January 20, 1951.

CHRONOLOGY OF REFERENCES

This study has made frequent reference to literary, theatrical, and graphic works by Jean Cocteau, to events in his life, and to quotations. We gather here, in chronological order, the works and certain events to which we have referred, inserting the principal films for the sake of reference.

1889   Birth of Jean Cocteau

1909   *La Lampe d'Aladin,* poems.

1910   Becomes close to Diaghilev, Nijinsky, Stravinsky.

1914   *Le Potomak,* poetic novel.

1915   *Discours du grand sommeil,* poetry. *Le Cap de Bonne-Espérance,* poetry (published in 1919). Acrobatic flights with Roland Garros, who is killed at the front shortly thereafter.

1916   Friendships: Picasso, Apollinaire, Max Jacob, Cendrars.

1918   Writes his adaptation of *Romeo et Juliette,* which was first performed in 1924. Accompanies Jean Wiener on the drums at the Gaya bar. *Le Coq et l'Arlequin,* critical poetry. Meets Radiguet.

1919   Articles appear in *Paris-Midi*: Subjects of his own choosing.

1921   *Les Mariés de la Tour Eiffel* (play.) Radiguet writes *Le Diable au corps* (Devil in the Flesh) during the vacation of the group of friends in Piquey (Arcachon).

1922   Writes his adaptations of *Antigone* and *Oedipus Rex*. Vacation at Pramousquier where Radiguet writes *Le Bal du comte d'Orgel,* and Cocteau writes *Le Grand Ecart,* novel; *Plain-Chant,* poem; *Thomas l'imposteur,* novel.

1923   Death of Radiguet, December 21.

1925   Writes the first poems of *Opéra, Orphée.* Publication of *L'Ange Heurtebise,* poem, and of *Le Mystère de Jean l'Oiseleur:* drawings.

1926   Writes for Stravinsky: *Oedipus-Rex.* June 17: premiere of *Orphée,* Pitoëff. *Le Rappel a l'Ordre,* critical poetry.

1928   Among his publications: *Le Livre blanc, Le Mystère laïc.* Preface to *J'adore* by Jean Desbordes.

1929   At the clinic in Saint-Cloud (second opium cure), and there writes *Les Enfants terribles* in 17 days.

1930   Reading of *La Voix humaine* at the Comédie-Française, February 17. April to September: filming of *The Blood of a Poet.* Moves to rue Vignon (Palais-Royal).

1932   January 20: premiere *The Blood of a Poet* at the Vieux-Colombier Theatre. Writes *La Machine infernale.*

1934   April 10: premiere of *La Machine infernale.*

1935–36   *Portraits-Souvenirs.*

1937   Column in the journal *Ce Soir.*
Les Chevaliers de la Table Ronde at the Théâtre de l'Oeuvre. Debut of Jean Marais.

1938   Writes *Les Parents terribles.* Premiere on November 14 at Les Ambassadeurs, then at Les Bouffes-Parisiens, after it had been banned by the City Council, owners of the first theatre.

1939   Writes *La Fin du Potomak* and *La Machine à écrire.*

1940   *Le Bel indifférent,* by Edith Piaf.

1941   Revival of *Les Parents terribles.* Fascist demonstrations against the play. Premiere of *La Machine à écrire,* banned. Writes *Renaud et Armide.* Articles for *Comœdia* (later collected in *Le Foyer des artistes*).

1942   Testifies in the defense of Jean Genêt. Works with Marcel Carné on an adaptation of *Juliette ou la clé des songes.*

1943   Premiere of *Renaud et Armide* at the Comédie-Française. Dialogues for *Le Baron fantôme.* Writes *L'Eternel Retour* and follows its presentation.

1944   Opening of *L'Eternel Retour*. *Léone,* poem. Death of Jean Desbordes after torture by the Gestapo.

1945   Dialogue for *Les Dames du Bois de Boulogne*. *La Belle et la Bête* (August to September). Publication of *Cocteau,* a study by Roger Lannes, in the Seghers collection "Poètes d'Aujourd'hui."

1946   Presentation of the ballet *Le Jeune Homme et la Mort* at the Théâtre des Champs-Elysées, opening of *La Belle et la Bête*. Wins the Prix Louis Delluc. *L'Aigle à deux têtes* is performed. *La Crucifixion,* poem.

1947   *La Voix humaine* is filmed by Rossellini. *Ruy Blas*. *L'Aigle à deux têtes*. *La Difficulté d'être*. Moves to Milly-la-Forêt.

1948   Openings of *Ruy Blas* and *L'Aigle à deux têtes*. Films *Les Parents terribles,* which opens in November. Commentary for *Les Noces de sable* by Zvoboda. Publication of the scenario of *The Blood of a Poet*. Sketch for the *Judith et Holopherne* tapestry.

1949   Organizes the *Festival du film maudit* at Biarritz. Preface for André Bazin's book on Orson Welles. Begins filming *Orpheus* in November.

1950   Follows the filming of *Les Enfants terribles*. *Orpheus* opens in Paris in September.

1951   *Entretiens autour du cinématographe* with André Fraigneau. Writes and speaks the commentary for *Le Rossignol de l'Empereur de Chine* by Jiri Trnka. Publication of his book on Jean Marais, 16 mm film on his frescoes in the villa of Santo-Sospir for Mme. Alec Weisweiller at Saint-Jean-Cap-Ferrat. *Bacchus* given at the Théâtre Marigny, attack by François Mauriac, reply by Cocteau.

1952   Writes *Journal d'un inconnu* (essays), published in 1953.

1953   Writes *La Dame à la licorne* (ballet).

1954   *Clair-Obscur,* poems. President of the jury for the Cannes Film Festival.

1955   March 3: elected to the Académie française.

1959   September: *Testament of Orpheus*.

1963   October 11: death of Jean Cocteau.